4

Tundra Teacher

Tundra Teacher

a memoir

by John Foley

EPICENTER PRESS
Alaska Book Adventures™

Epicenter Press is a regional press founded in Alaska whose interests include but are not limited to the arts, history, environment, and diverse cultures and lifestyles of the Pacific Northwest and high latitudes. We seek both the traditional and innovative in publishing nonfiction books, and contemporary art and photography gift books.

Publisher: Kent Sturgis
Cover and Book Design: Victoria Sturgis
Map: Marge Mueller, Gray Mouse Graphics
Proofreader: Sherrill Carlson
Printer: Transcontinental Printing Co.

Library of Congress Control Number: 2003108042

ISBN 0-9724944-1-3

Booksellers: This title is available from major wholesalers. Retail discounts are available from our trade distributor, Graphic Arts Center Publishing Co., PO Box 10306, Portland, OR 97210. Phone 800-452-3032.

PRINTED IN CANADA

First Edition
First Printing, July 2003

10 9 8 7 6 5 4 3 2 1

To order single copies of TUNDRA TEACHER, mail $14.95 plus $4.95 for shipping (WA residents add $1.30 state sales tax) to: Epicenter Press, PO Box 82368, Kenmore, WA 98028.

Discover exciting ALASKA BOOK ADVENTURES! Visit our online Alaska bookstore at www.EpicenterPress.com, or call our 24-hour, toll-free hotline at 800-950-6663. Visit our online gallery for Iditarod artist Jon Van Zyle at www.JonVanZyle.com.

For Rod Boyce & Julie Stricker, Fern & Ann Chandonnet, and Bounders Hither & Yon.

Preface

I never wanted to write an "Alaskan Adventure" book. You've seen the type—a guy shoots a few unarmed animals or climbs the steep side of a mountain and writes a tale of triumph. This book, on the other hand, started as a collection of Alaska stories, which seemed a more noble endeavor. The stories I wrote were true, although at times I was tempted to go beyond the "slinking facts of life," as Don Marquis put it, and "tell a few stretchers," as Mark Twain put it.

Eventually I was persuaded to keep the honesty and make the book more chronological and cohesive, focusing on my experiences as a newspaper reporter and Bush teacher.

However you classify it, this particular Alaska story began in late 1989. I'd always been curious about the 49th state and I was restless and bored in the Chicago suburbs. More significantly, a beautiful woman broke off her engagement to me, I was heartbroken, and it was either the Last Frontier or the French Foreign Legion. . .

Introduction

I wasn't a teacher when I moved to Alaska, although I'd been considering a career change for a while. I entered graduate school in Anchorage after almost two years at the *Anchorage Times*. Earning a teaching degree was costly and time-consuming, and I kicked myself for not taking the requisite courses as an undergraduate. (I had majored in political science, for reasons that have since escaped me.) Looking back now, however, I'm grateful for my ten years as a newspaper reporter. I met amazing people —some as colleagues and some as story subjects—and I was given enough freedom to develop my own writing style. I'd also seen much of human nature and had some great stories by the time I stepped into the classroom, all of which has been invaluable.

Overall, I enjoy teaching more than reporting—a well-taught lesson is more rewarding for me than a well-written news story, and I'll take hassles from a smart-ass kid over a boring municipal meeting any day. Yet, I think about my newspaper career every time I prepare a lesson, which I generally do at the last minute, to simulate the deadline pressure that I came to enjoy.

Unfortunately, there is no way to simulate the dedication of purpose in a newsroom. Teachers spend more of their working hours in their own classrooms, so you don't get to hear your colleagues laugh and boast, yell and cry, piss and moan—except occasionally at lunch. And, while teachers are, on the whole, more caring and positive than newspaper folks I know, sometimes I miss the company of those self-centered and cynical bastards.

Changes in Latitudes

1

When the newspaper asked me to jump out of an airplane I should have known I was falling out of favor.

Once arrived I went to work as a reporter for *The Anchorage Times*, which had been revitalized by VECO (which had something to do with Big Oil). Initially, I also wrote a couple of columns a week. Subjects included a cookie-munching moose in my neighborhood, a picture-painting elephant in the zoo, a boat-eating fish in Lake Iliamna, and other important wildlife issues.

We were engaged in a newspaper war with *The Anchorage Daily News*, and things were testy between editorial staffers on the two papers. Still, there were some acts of graciousness. When *Times* photographer Russ Kendall had his equipment stolen from his car, for example, some photographers from the *Daily News* lent him their equipment. And the *Times* staff sent flowers when a *Daily News* editor unexpectedly passed away.

There was some divisiveness at *The Times*, especially between the veteran staffers and those of us brought in from Outside by VECO. Still, the competition with *The Daily News* and the passage of time helped unite us, and we often went out in large groups for movies and post-deadline beers.

The unstable tectonic nature of the Anchorage area was revealed to some of us when we gathered to watch *Dances With Wolves* at a local theater. As the buffalo were stampeding on the screen, we began to shake violently in our seats, and one of my colleagues yelled, "Now THAT'S a special effect!"

Another solidifying occasion was the bachelor party for fellow columnist Jeff Houck. I helped put the event together on a Friday night, despite having a reporting assignment in Girdwood early Saturday morning.

The party was a success; the highlight was probably the lap dance we purchased for a cub reporter fresh from the farmlands of Indiana, who blushed so deeply we thought he might be having a heart attack.

I drove straight from the strip club to Girdwood. I'd stopped drinking hours earlier but was in that vague state of unease caused by alcohol-consumption and sleep-deprivation. My assignment was to interview some folks with the Alyeska Skydivers and jump out of a plane. I suppose this assignment should have tipped me off that I was falling out of favor at *The Times*.

I enjoyed my job as a feature writer, for the most part, primarily because I've always been curious about people leading interesting lives and the motivation that drives them. Reporters who specialize in such "soft" news are not generally prized as much as "hard" news reporters, and I think this is partly why I went into a free-fall at *The Times*. I'm biased, of course, but I've never understood why hard news is so appealing to newspaper editors. Consider your basic scandal: a politician is caught using taxpayer funds for, say, a vacation to Mexico with a woman other than his wife. This is front page stuff, and the reporter who catches the unlucky lecher is lauded as the next Woodward and/or Bernstein. But why? We all know politicians lie, steal and Lewinsky, so why is it newsworthy when they are inevitably caught?

In any case, I was the go-to guy at *The Times* for strange profiles and personal experience stories, which more or less explains why I jumped out of the aforementioned plane.

Also jumping that morning were three young women, Sarah Darling, Susy Weiss and Natalie Bare, friends working in Alaska for the summer. All of us were going to tandem jump, a style in which an instructor is harnessed to the novice.

I zipped into a colorful jumpsuit and received some basic instructions. My concentration wasn't good for obvious reasons. I was also in a cynical mood as I considered Jeff facing the bold new world of marriage: he was getting married, I was throwing myself out of a plane. There was, I thought, a certain symmetry to our actions.

We climbed aboard a Cessna 182. Darling's tandem instructor was Bob Johns, president of the club, and my instructor was Tim Robel. We took off and pilot Bill Dau pointed the plane south.

The turquoise-white glaciers, craggy mountains and deep blue waters that compose the quilt of Alaska helped take my mind off the pain in my head and legs. I was kneeling on the hard floor of the plane so Robel could attach the harness. I have bad knees anyway and the pain slowly turned to agony.

Dau saw my discomfort. "Get 'em on their knees for a while," he said, "and it's one of the things that helps persuade people to jump."

We turned southeast, gaining altitude. Below, a trio of power boats and their following wakes looked like arrows shooting across Prince William Sound. We turned north and Denali and Foraker came into view, monoliths on the horizon.

We were at nine-thousand feet and heading west back toward Girdwood. Robel opened the door and, following instructions, I stepped out on the small foothold, hanging onto the wing brace. Robel gave me the signal and before I thought about it, I jumped.

Then I thought about it. I JUMPED OUT OF A PLANE! For a second I was paralyzed with fear; then I recalled instructions and went into a belly-flop arch. I watched the altimeter on my chest during the free fall and, still following instructions, signaled Robel when we were at fifty-five hundred feet.

Very good, I didn't forget. What a bright fellow I am and how collected under pressure, despite lack of sleep and the aforementioned semi-hangover. Now what? Hmm. Seemed there was something else I was supposed to do...Ah yes, pull the parachute cord.

We were dropping at about 120 mph, and by the time I reached for the cord we had lost another one thousand feet. Robel beat me to the pull.

Suddenly the hurricane-like wind stopped blowing past and the world was quiet, even serene. Above us I saw Sarah Darling – actually I heard her screaming first – and then saw her chute open. The bright, lumpy parachutes resembled a collection of balloons.

Robel showed me how to turn the chute with the handgrips. We did a 360-degree spin and I felt nauseated, but the rest of the trip was a joy, gliding along and watching the verdant earth come slowly into focus.

We landed in a marshy field next to Girdwood airport. Clumsily, I fell to my knees and over on my side. Darling and Johns made a cleaner landing a moment later.

"That was incredible," said Darling, her face flushed with excitement. "Your senses are so heightened, I remember everything I did. I definitely have got to do that again."

Once was enough for me.

During these early days in Alaska I shared a house with Mike Taylor, an excellent sportswriter at the paper. We both enjoyed books, basketball and beer, and naturally became friends.

Mike and I also shared a minimalist attitude toward house cleaning. Cleanliness, however, is next to Godliness only in some cases, because while our house was a mess, it seemed to be held in special favor by the Almighty. Everyone who visited agreed on this point. A visitor would look around at the crumb-covered furniture, the mountains of newspapers, the decorative beer cans, the piles of pizza boxes, and typically declare, "OH MY GOD!" Sometimes the visitor said, "JESUS CHRIST!" Often the visitor never returned.

The smell was a contributing culprit. Some of the newspapers, you see, contained droppings from Mike's beloved but untrained mutt, Zeus. Although I was accustomed to the odor, sometimes it became too much even for me, and I would need to head out for a cross-country ski or a hike in the mountains. As I left the house I'd often "accidentally" forget to shut the front door, which, despite our collective lack of valuables, annoyed Mike. My view was that the place needed airing and God should be able to come and go as He pleased.

Less than a year into my first year at *The Times* I was demoted from Feature Writer/Columnist to Arts Editor. I didn't like the new position as well, although I did get to interview some interesting show biz folks who came through Anchorage, including Jay Leno and James Earl Jones. Leno was very gracious and helpful, although he was eating something during our phone interview; I didn't want to ask him and have him hang up, but a good guess is a cheeseburger because it sounded juicy. Jones, on the other hand, hung up on me after about two minutes because I had the temerity to ask him about his famous voice. "What do you *mean* I have a famous voice?" he thundered in his Darth Vader baritone. Then I heard a click.

I liked meeting the cast and crew of *Salmonberries*, a film shot in Kotzebue. I thought the director, Percy Adlon, was trying to create some creative friction by casting k.d. lang, the Canadian singer-songwriter-vegetarian-PETA spokesperson, and Chuck Conners, the politically incorrect-former jock-former "Rifleman"-ardent carnivore. Conners liked to joke that he needed his eggs basted with bacon grease for the sake of his heart.

I first met Conners at Anchorage International Airport. During the subsequent interview he said he was interested in working with Adlon because he admired a previous film, *Baghdad Cafe*. Afterward, Conners asked me to help direct him to the right plane. I walked with him to the gate, and when he saw the plane was headed to Nome, he turned to me in shock. "Nome? You're trying to send me to *Nome*, pal?" I explained that he'd fly through Nome to get to Kotzebue, which was further north – above the Arctic Circle. "North of Nome," he said, shaking his head.

I went up to Kotzebue a few days later. It was fascinating to watch the filming process, and I had interesting interviews with lang and Adlon, both of whom struck me as very committed artists. I did not enjoy meeting some crew members and reporters, all from Los Angeles, who seemed intent on criticizing Alaska in general and Kotzebue in particular. Some of them were incapable of uttering a sentence without heavy sarcasm. And in general they had a hipper-than-thou attitude that was annoying. When a snowball fight broke out at a party, I took pleasure in aiming a few missiles in their direction. The party, incidentally, included lots of other white powder as well.

One crew member I did like was the set manager from Australia. We got to talking one morning at breakfast, and he said he moved to Los Angeles from his homeland a year earlier — and was absolutely miserable. He didn't like the walls people put up between themselves and others in L.A. based on status, wealth, race and other factors. In a short time he felt utterly disconnected from what he had hoped would be his new community, and one morning sat down, put his head in his hands and cried. A friend recommended that he try Alaska, where the land was lovely and the people genuine. He'd been in the state a few months, he said, landed the job on *Salmonberries*, and never planned to leave.

2

The prospect of a cold beer comforted me, encouraged me,
and possibly saved my life.

More than anything, hiking in the mountains seemed to restore my soul in the aftermath of my Chicago breakup. I went through the usual phases of anger and regret; replayed scenes of my former fiancee, both good and bad; and bored new friends with my tale of woe.

Perhaps I should have sought counseling; I sought the high places instead, and gradually this seemed to work. I'm not sure why – initially I just sensed that being in the mountains was good for me. I enjoyed the physical challenge, the views, and the quiet.

While I'd climbed quite a few mountains on various vacations and journeys before moving to Alaska, I'd never lived near the mountains until I moved to Anchorage. The Chugach is a beautiful range, austere yet inviting, and I was a figure of fun sometimes when I'd gaze with rapt attention at the front range outside of town – like a tourist in New York looking up at the tall buildings.

The mountains in the distance soon became the mountains around me and above me and – when conditions permitted – below me. Starting out I was a consummate peak-bagger, striving to "conquer" mountains rather than just be among them. I made some novice mistakes that I was lucky to survive, most notably a solo attempt of East Twin Peak in November. I scrambled up a dangerous wall and on the descent became chilled in my improvised clothing. Exhausted afterward, I almost drove my car into a tree on the ice-covered road near Lake Eklutna.

But there were moments of grace, too. One March morning I climbed through a cold cobalt blue shadow into a warm and dazzling world of white. One June afternoon I scrambled to a summit and found an unlikely throne of grass. I sat and listened to the silence and felt the stillness. In blissful meditation I watched the day unfold below.

The return to Anchorage was typically bittersweet. I'd drop my pack and ice axe inside the door and sink into a bathtub with the hottest water I could stand. I'd sip a beer, listen to Mozart, and feel my body slowly recover from the physical exertions I imposed in the cause of soul repair. And for a while I would be at peace.

Quite a few of us at *The Times* took to the outdoors during our free time. I enjoyed a solitary hike or ski, but it was always more pleasurable with company, and so I was pleased to meet Fern Chandonnet at the paper. Fern was a demanding copy editor known as "the word bully" for his extensive vocabulary, exquisite usage and enthusiastic opinions. He also wrote the humorous "Dear Bud" column, and he enjoyed climbing and skiing in his spare time.

Fern was kind enough to lead me and several other *Times* greenhorns on hikes through the Chugach. Outings became more frequent as we all became friends, and we would usually go climbing, hiking or skiing once or twice a week.

Actually, I only went hiking and skiing. I tried rock climbing a few times, but had an epiphany one day when I was clinging to a sheer face with my foot twitching and a harness digging into my crotch. "I'm just a hiker!" I declared.

Know thyself, the sages counsel.

Anyway, I'm not sure who dubbed us "The Down and Outward Bounders." I do recall that we all liked the name, not only because of the play on the Outward Bound wilderness school, but because it described the arc we'd follow if we fell on some of our climbs, and the economic status of most newspaper journalists.

It wasn't long before we had a dozen or so Down and Outward Bounders – Bounders, for short – with about as many associate members. Associates became full-fledged Bounders when they scaled a challenging mountain, or did something else in the wilderness to prove themselves worthy of Bounderhood. For example, Jeff Houck attained full Bounder status when he scaled Little O'Malley peak. We believe this was the first ascent by a two-hundred-seventy-five-pounder.

Because Bounders were average athletes and not always fit, we suffered on long outings. More than six or seven hours of climbing generally produced a condition we called Bounder Delirium, or B.D. for short.

B.D. symptoms included dazed looks, bad jokes and stating the obvious. Typically, after hiking through a downpour for several hours, Bounder Rod would look about, mystified, and announce: "It's raining." My tendency was to reach a summit and declare the scene remarkable, fabulous, amazing and the other thesaurus entries relating to wonderful, until another Bounder told me to shut up.

We talked about forming bylaws prohibiting such frowned-upon behavior as running, singing or flower-picking. We discussed a pledge calling for us to "rejoice in the discomfort of other hikers (i.e., "Communists")." And we decided our motto should be: "Every man for himself."

Some of our "bylaws" were subject to interpretation. If, for example, you couldn't hold a tune, could the noise you produced really be considered singing? And is jogging down a scree slope the same as running? The most important Bounder bylaw – "Bounders don't whine" – was the most frequently debated. A Bounder might stop and declare: "My feet hurt, my clothes are wet, this pace is too fast, and your conversation is liberal drivel." Is this whining? Or a statement of fact?

Bounder Fern was a strict constructionist when it came to the bylaws, most likely because — as Bounder Rod Boyce put it – Fern is old. But to his credit, Fern did little whining himself. The one time it would have been excused was when he fell and injured himself while descending from the summit of Ptarmigan Peak, a knotty, pyramidal mountain south of Anchorage.

He tripped while heading down a snow-covered gully with about a forty-degree slope. In an instant he was tumbling toward some rocks. He managed to roll over on his stomach and execute a self-arrest with his ice axe to stop himself—just short of the rocks. He badly sprained his ankle in the process, however, and with four miles of rugged hiking to go, some whining would have been understandable. Fern just limped back to the trailhead.

In keeping with the Bounder spirit, we reminded him of his ungainly fall rather than his textbook self-arrest and admirable stoicism. He expected no less from Bounders; this was not a club dedicated to enhancing self-esteem.

Of course not everyone understood or appreciated the Bounders. I found this out when I invited a friend to join us on a climb of Pioneer Peak in the Matanuska Valley.

After we reached the summit, I made my usual declarations about Beauty, and we started down. I was very tired and made an error in judgment; I should have stayed on the ridge, but decided a traverse between ridges would be quicker and easier. Rod decided to follow along, while Fern and my friend remained on the ridge.

On our descent fatigue made me sloppy, and I accidentally kicked a rock down towards Rod, who was about twenty yards below me. Okay, it was more of a boulder. I yelled a warning and he nimbly stepped aside. I apologized but naturally, as a Bounder, he has never let me forget that I almost killed him with a rock – and he doesn't walk in front of me anymore, either.

I was in the latter stages of Bounder Delirium when we finally reached the ridge. Fern dubbed our effort "The Dufus Traverse." Rod, though tired, was feeling well enough to continue down immediately, while I rested awhile with my non-Bounding friend. For some reason, he picked this time to deliver a sermon on the evils of alcohol.

As a counselor, he had seen firsthand the damage wrought by alcohol. He said folks would never drink or go into a bar if they considered all the tragic consequences that could follow. He was right, of course, but I argued the case for drinking in moderation.

I felt compelled to make this argument for two reasons. First, I was exhausted, and over the last few hours the thought of a cold beer had comforted me, encouraged me, and possibly saved my life.

Then, too, I knew my fellow Bounders, now well ahead on the trail, were undoubtedly celebrating the climb with a few drinks, and I didn't want my teetotaler friend to be surprised by the sight.

My plan failed. At the trailhead, Bounder Fern approached us waving a bottle of port, and behind him we could see Bounder Rod passed out under a tree. So much for moderation.

My counselor friend declined to join us on future climbs.

No, the Bounders did not make the best impression on everyone, and we could, in truth, be a rather cynical and critical bunch. Yet perhaps that was what made the Bounders special. These days there are too many self-congratulatory clubs, too many huggy support groups. We need fewer compliments and more cruel, honest criticism. Don't most of us cringe when complimented, anyway? Or brace for a sales pitch? It seems to me that friendship has more to do with giving and taking grief.

Not that the Bounders were constantly critical. Sometimes we were nice to each other. Bounders Rod and Julie liked each other so much they got married.

The wedding was held on a bluff overlooking Turnagain Arm, and included ice axes, hiking boots and a pod of beluga whales that surfaced, as if on cue, shortly before the "man and wife" pronouncement.

Bounder Fern served as minister at the ceremony. This was somewhat ironic because despite seeing Jesus Christ when he visited my house, he's not at all religious. In fact, he has been known to curse the mountain gods and send crosses spiraling off summits. Yet, for all that, Fern and the other Bounders have tremendous spirit, and it was my good fortune to meet them at *The Times* and share their company.

3

My father — management consultant and bear bait.

My family never completely understood why I moved to Alaska. I would tell them about the beauty of the land, and climbing in the mountains, and meeting unusual and interesting people, and they would encourage me to move back to "someplace normal."

My youngest brother Brian, fresh out of high school, was the first member of my family to venture north. We had fun exploring the wilderness together, but it quickly became apparent that he needed direction and motivation. When I was busy working, his typical day in Anchorage was to rise at the crack of noon, watch TV for a few hours, and cruise around town in the evening.

Naturally, I arranged for him to work on a fishing boat.

Our mother Barbara got wind of the plan, and while she agreed that Brian needed a kick in the pants, she also made it clear that if anything happened to her sixth and youngest child, I would be unwelcome at future family gatherings, and best find a good hiding place.

Something did happen to Brian: He worked ridiculous hours on a processor in the Bering Sea, had a close encounter with a shark while sorting fish belowdecks, lost all his baby fat, got into a fistfight on the dock in Seward, made a wad of cash, and felt much better about himself and his future.

We took a long hike in the mountains when he returned to Anchorage. As we neared the trailhead on the return, we saw a man trying to place his toddler on the back of a moose, while the mother prepared to capture the moment with a camera.

Brian and I looked at each other, then warned the family that moose could be dangerous. They ignored our advice. Remarkably, the moose accepted this invasion of privacy without becoming violent.

I'd seen this Disney Syndrome up close a few other times. In Kincaid Park in Anchorage, for example, I saw a man pick a fight with another moose he must have mistaken for Bullwinkle.

I was skiing with my friend Fern when we spotted the moose, munching on a tree and blocking the trail. While we stood there discussing strategy, another skier came huffing up the trail. He passed us with a sneer on his face, as if to say, "Real men don't fear moose."

"You know," Fern said as we watched the man ski toward his fate, "I'll bet that moose weighs twelve-hundred pounds."

"At least," I agreed.

"What would you think if you walked into a bar and saw a twelve-hundred-pound guy sitting there?"

"Sturdy bar stools?"

"That's not the point, young John. The point is, would you pick a fight with a twelve-hundred-pound guy?"

"Definitely not."

We watched as the skier neared the moose. The moose turned toward him with a torpid expression. Then, like any self-respecting twelve-hundred-pound guy whose space is invaded, the moose charged.

The man fell down and raised his arm to fend off the moose, who stood over him and seemed to debate whether to stomp him or not. "Help!" the man yelled to us – the guys he just insulted.

"Crawl behind a tree," Fern advised. "A big one."

The man followed directions and was soon out of stomping range. The moose that spared him wandered off, leaving us to complete our ski. As we passed the shaken skier, Fern yelled, "Damn Communist, show some respect!"

Why is it, we wondered, that otherwise intelligent people become dumb and dumber in the wilderness? Sometimes I agreed with Fern that we should rid the gene pool of the folks by enticing them with unique wilderness opportunities: Pet a polar bear in Barrow! Ride a moose in the Matanuska! Split a salmon sandwich with a Kenai griz! In a way, this would be a public service; and if the victims survived, they would learn that in Alaska, reality *really* bites.

The problem with this plan is that it would, in all likelihood, eliminate some of my own family members. My father in particular comes to mind. I persuaded the old man to visit Alaska soon after Brian returned from the fishing boat. Joining him were my brother Mike, my sister Mary, and her husband, Dave.

Dave and Mary went off on a cruise of Prince William Sound, where they discovered Alaska's direct brand of humor. It was cold on the deck of the ship, naturally, and Mary, within earshot of an Alaskan guide, noted that it was probably a result of the elevation. "Oh yes," the guide agreed, "it's ten feet above sea level on the lower deck, but twenty feet on the upper!" In Whittier they went to a cafe where Dave, an accountant, noted a sign that read, "No fucking checks!" Below this was a returned check and another sign that read, "A fucking check!"

Meanwhile, I made the mistake of taking the old man camping on the Crow Pass Trail, along with Mike and Brian. Trouble was in the air when Dad insisted on strapping his reclining lawn chair onto Mike's pack and using his beloved old shillelagh as a walking stick.

We hiked down the trail a few miles and camped next to Eagle River. We had a stunning view of the mountains, but I knew my father, who grew up in New York City, was underwhelmed when he looked around and said, "Doesn't anyone cut the grass around here?"

Soon after we ran out of marshmallows, we had to resolve the tent issue. I had the choice of sharing my tent with Brian, who snores like a garbage disposal, or with Dad, who vilifies camping while extolling the virtues of civilization. I chose Dad.

Right off he insisted on bringing his lawn chair into the tent. I told him I had a pad all set up, but he insisted that he'd be more comfortable in his chair. And he was okay for about an hour. Then he bolted upright so quickly his chair collapsed under him. The long hike had left him with one of the worst things that can happen in a crowded tent: leg cramp.

Dear ol' Dad ripped his way outside and limped around in a circle, cussing tents, hiking, camping, nature in general and Alaska in particular. He yanked his chair out of the tent, saying he was going to sleep outside. I thought he meant just outside the tent, so I dozed off thinking he'd be fine. When nature called later that night, however, I looked around and saw that he'd parked his reclining lawn chair directly beneath our food cache.

My father, management consultant and bear bait.

I woke Mike and we went over to talk to him. We urged him to give the tent another try. When he refused, Mike pointed at the bundle of food hanging precariously over his head. "If a bear doesn't get you," he said, "the pilot bread might."

"I'm not afraid of bears," he said. "I have my shillelagh." I mentioned that a grizzly could use his shillelagh as a toothpick. Still, he refused to budge, so Mike handed him a can of pepper spray bear repellent. "Don't let the brown bears bite," he said. We discussed our inheritance on the way back to our tents.

The next morning, when I climbed out of my tent, I saw my father using Mike's pepper spray like bug repellent. "This doesn't work at all," he said. Afterward, while the old man was bemoaning the lack of newspaper and coffee stands in the area, I decided that in the future I would avoid forcing my wilderness pleasures on others; clearly, some folks are better off in a hotel with a Disney movie.

4

A happy smile born of hope that comes with starting
over once again.

I met a lovely woman named Amy Durgeloh about a
year after arriving in Alaska. By this time I had worked
my way down the ladder to general assignment reporter,
and I was assigned to check out flooding in a section of
Anchorage near a river. One of the buildings affected
was occupied by the Anchorage Opera, where Amy
worked. We talked, we smiled, we fell.

Part of my initial attraction to Amy was that she was so
completely different than the other women I dated at the
time — which was a good thing. My Chicago fiancee, for example, liked to get stoned with a half-dozen of her male
college friends on an all too-frequent basis; and an Anchorage girlfriend liked to dress in what she termed her "Dangerous Bitch" outfit and scare people at local taverns. Such
behavior does not lend itself to a contented relationship.

Amy, on the other hand, was sweet, religious, close to
her family, down-to-earth — and always tastefully dressed.
As a costume designer for the opera, she liked to joke that

while she might not know the details of a particular histori-cal period, she knew what they were wearing. I knew Amy was good for me and dove enthusiastically into the relation-ship; we discussed marriage after dating only a month.

The problem was that, against all logic, I was still carry-ing a flame for my Chicago fiancee. So after my initial en-thusiasm, I failed to put my whole heart and soul into the relationship with Amy, as she deserved.

I also had doubts as to whether I was the marrying sort. I'm a total slob, as stated earlier, not to mention unhandy around the house (or in the house, for that matter), fre-quently restless, annoyingly impulsive, occasionally drunk, perpetually short of funds, and habitually self-in-volved. Such qualities do not lend themselves to a con-tented relationship.

These were among the reasons I left Amy and headed down the Alaska Highway in September 1991. The long run down to Seattle warmed my cold feet and eased my doubts somewhat, and I called Amy. Naturally, she was quite up-set, and it was made worse because her family members were not around to comfort her. She said they were hunting.

"For me?" I asked.

"No, for caribou," she replied. "But you're next."

I decided to return to Anchorage.

My primary problem on the return trip was finances. I was running low on cash, didn't want to ask Amy for money, and had recently shredded all my credit cards except the one over the limit. So I began selling off my possessions at secondhand stores in Canada. A portable stereo yielded twenty dollars in Cache Creek. A blanket brought five more in Prince George. And a store owner in Fort St. John paid fifteen dollars for my ice axe.

"Ya hey, I think I'll kill my wife with this," he said, hefting the axe with a smile.

Canadian humor.

My luck ran out in the Yukon Territory. A rear tire blew, sending a death rattle through the steering wheel. I pulled over in the middle of nowhere and replaced the flat with one of those spares about the size of a mountain bike tire, the ones that come with a warning label on the side and cause the car to sag in one corner.

The warning label on this tire said to drive no more than thirty miles and keep the speed below thirty-five mph. So I limped on toward the Alaska border, calculating how long it would take to reach Anchorage at my new pace. On the outskirts of Haines Junction, I passed a hitchhiker holding a sign with one word: "Alaska." My car was brimming with all my worldly belongings and I wasn't in the mood for small talk, but he looked so forlorn that I turned around.

Rolling down my window, I explained that I couldn't drive fast on my spare tire, and he might have better luck waiting for an uninjured vehicle.

"I've been standing here three days," he said. "I'll get to the border faster with you."

With a sigh I pulled over and cleared out the front passenger seat. The back seat now looked like an avalanche hazard, and he had to keep his backpack in front, jammed against his knees. He thanked me profusely and we exchanged names. I must admit I've since forgotten his.

He appeared to be in his late 20s and he had dirty blond hair, which might have been light blond when clean. He said he'd been camping out for 10 days while hitching up to Alaska from Montana, and was surprised he didn't really smell bad yet.

"That's a matter of opinion," I laughed. "You get used to your own odor when you camp out, so you don't think you smell bad even when you do." I added that I spoke from personal experience as a fellow camper and hitchhiker. Still, he seemed slightly offended.

We spent most of the next fifty miles admiring the St. Elias Mountains looming directly in front of us. Every few miles I remembered my spare and slowed to under thirty-five mph. The hitchhiker told me a little about himself. He said he lost his job as a cook and was arrested for a drug-related offense, and was heading to Alaska to start fresh. It's a rather common story, of course – fleeing to the end of the Earth to remake oneself. Still, the underlying reasons are compelling to the individual, the tales always slightly different, and I usually find them quite moving.

When it was my turn to explain what I was doing on the Alaska Highway, it was his turn to laugh.

By this time the hitchhiker and I were closing in on the Alaska border. He was excited, and let out a rebel yell when we entered the state. The spare tire was wobbling and obviously not planning to make Anchorage, so in Northway I purchased a used tire, regular size, for fifteen bucks. Meanwhile, the hitchhiker called his father and arranged to have one hundred dollars sent to him in Palmer. He said he had a friend there who was going to put him up for a while and get him a job as a commercial fisherman.

It was invigorating to travel at relatively high speeds again. The sun had set, we were tired, but both of us wanted to keep going straight through. On the winding section of the Glenn Highway north of Sutton, fatigue began to tell. I was nodding off for a second or two, then snapping to terrified attention as the car drifted toward one precipitous drop or another. The hitchhiker, plastered to the death seat, decided to help by talking loudly about his four ex-wives and experiences playing guitar in a rock band.

I dropped him in front of a bar in Palmer at 4 a.m. Somehow I managed to stay awake for the last hour of my five-thousand-mile trek, and pulled safely into Anchorage. I was married to Amy in November, became busy with school and work, and all but forgot about my hitchhiking acquaintance.

Our paths crossed again in late April, almost eight months after we first met. I was returning from a night class in Eagle River and, fittingly enough, he was hitchhiking on the ramp heading to Anchorage. We said what you say about coincidence and gave each other the short version of our lives since September. I was embarrassed at not recalling his name, but he didn't seem to recall mine, either.

He said he was in Fairbanks all winter, but recently had lost his job and girlfriend. So he was heading to Homer to work in a cannery. The commercial fishing job didn't come up.

I noticed he looked visibly older, with deep-set lines around his eyes. And I saw that he wasn't carrying anything but a bag of chocolate-chip cookies. He said his backpack was stolen while he was in a bar the day before.

While traveling, he was sleeping on the roadside, and his biggest concern was becoming some grizzly's dinner. I thought cold might be more of a problem. I drove him as far as Girdwood and gave him an old blanket I had in the trunk.

As I drove off, I saw him in the rear-view mirror: standing in the emergency lane, blanket about his shoulders, thumb held high and, surprisingly, a wide smile on his face. Of course it could have been an act to beguile motorists, but I like to think it was just a happy smile, born of the hope that comes with starting over once again.

When I left Amy to head to Seattle, I also left my job at *The Times*. In truth, there wasn't much of a job to leave — I had worked my way down to General Assignment Reporter, and mostly wrote leftover barely-news, the police blotter and obituaries. It was, to say the least, a dead-end job.

Anyway, I was unemployed upon my return, and I decided it would be a fine time to change careers to teaching. I've always enjoyed discussing literature and writing, and teaching seemed a more noble and altruistic profession: your entire objective is to help young people learn. Journalism can also be a noble (and sometimes ignoble) profession. Over the years I'd done my share of "weeping widow" stories, which required me to ingratiate myself with a victim's family, make sympathetic noises, and ask probing personal questions until I had enough quotable material.

No more—I said good-bye to all that and signed up for a full load of teaching classes at the University of Alaska Anchorage. I also worked several part-time jobs. My first, driving a cab, did not work out as I had hoped; I made fouteen bucks in twelve hours my first day and had a close encounter with a mugger, so opted instead for the consistent pay of a bus driver.

I thought driving a school bus would be excellent preparation for teaching. It helped a bit, I suppose, but I soon learned that the most effective way to maintain order on the bus is to stop the vehicle, while the most effective way to maintaining discipline in a classroom is to take charge and, if necessary, yell. Physically disciplining students also works well, but is frowned upon these days. So, we must learn what *motivates* the foul-mouthed mauler, we must *reason* with the rude ruffian, we must, above all, discipline with *dignity*. In my opinion, the ruler-wielding nuns of my youth had a better approach.

One morning on my bus route the roads were in terrible shape. I'm a slow driver anyway, so I had no problem on my first run to Dimond High School. After dropping off the kids, I was chugging down a nearby hill, and my brakes failed. I was on a patch of ice and slowly drifting toward a car at a traffic light. The driver saw me coming, but cross traffic prevented him from moving, and I slowly crashed the bus into the rear of his vehicle.

A cop gave me a ticket for reckless driving, and my co-workers gave me crap. "So, how *were* things over at Dimond this morning?" they asked on the afternoon run.

While I was underemployed, my friends at *The Times* were soon unemployed; the paper folded on June 3, 1992. While I did not enjoy my last position at the paper, I naturally felt bad for my friends and former colleagues who had fought the good fight and were suddenly jobless. A poignant photo of Rod Boyce was featured on the final front page — arms crossed, head-bowed, being comforted by another grieving staff member. Mike Taylor, for his part, wrote a farewell sports column that seamlessly blended humor and pathos in a way that would have made Red Smith proud. And Fern Chandonnet declared, "It wasn't my fault!"

I did well in my classes at the University of Alaska, and began student-teaching at Service High School in Anchorage in January, 1993. I found that generally I was a bit looser than most beginning teachers; I liked telling jokes and anecdotes, and my objective, then and now, was to make the learning experience enjoyable. This philosophy served me well from day one, and I developed a quick rapport with my classes at Service.

It was interesting that I was told at the University not to go too in-depth with Shakespeare's *Romeo and Juliet* because the puns and double entendres were sexually suggestive. Then I worked with Ellen Kennedy, an experienced and progressive teacher at Service High, and she thought we should explain exactly what Shakespeare meant beyond the obvious by such phrases as "draw thy tool" and "my naked weapon is out."

Student interest perked up immediately, and I learned that linking literature to student experience – or unsavory curiosity – was the best way to keep them engaged. Of course, sometimes student interest became almost too keen, as when we reached the part of the play when Mercutio was teasing his friend Romeo about Rosaline, the object of his affection before Juliet. At one point Mercutio says, "O, that she were an open-arse, thou a poperin pear!"

"What's that mean?" a student asked before I could move along.

I looked over at Ellen working at her desk; she smiled and shrugged, and so I boldly went where perhaps no student-teacher had ever gone before: "Well," I said, "a poperin pear is phallic-shaped, so Mercutio was suggesting that Romeo, um...have anal intercourse with his girlfriend."

That woke 'em up in the back row.

"Dude!"

"Awesome!"

"Is a poperin pear shaped like a banana?"

They were riveted to the text for the remainder of the play, and were profoundly saddened when Mercutio – Shakespeare's most lecherous character – died in a sword fight.

While Ellen had no trouble retaking control of her class when my student teaching duties were completed in May, the other teacher I worked with at Service might have had a few problems. The day I left, a student handed me a card signed by the entire class. It wished me luck and added: "Don't go, Mr. Foley! You can't leave us with that bitch!"

5

Whisky, I've learned has played a prominent role in most of Alaska's historic events.

That summer, when time permitted, Amy and I took some nice trips around the state. On the Fourth of July, I decided to participate in the annual Mount Marathon race in Seward, which Mike Taylor and Amy's brother Mac both extolled as a truly unique Alaskan experience.

Basically, on a day traditionally reserved for beer and barbecues, several hundred men and women risk life and limb by running up and down the mountain, a 3,022-foot peak overlooking Seward. Thousands more gather to witness the annual carnage. Most are clustered at the base of the mountain, which, like a curve at the Indianapolis 500, is the best place to see a crash.

Curiosity prompted me to do some formal research on this spectacle, so I read musty old newspapers, interviewed a couple of runner-crashers, and hung out in bars. This was appropriate because the Mount Marathon race was born in a Seward bar. As the story goes, some old-timers hatched the plan over drinks. Whisky, I've learned, has played a prominent role in most of Alaska's historic events.

On the day of the race, the judges outnumbered the participants, but when the rocks stopped tumbling, Jim Walter was the winner in one hour and two minutes.

My research included participating in the race. I weighed about two-hundred-forty pounds at the time, which I thought entitled me to a handicap of sorts. How else could I hope to compete with those tiny runners?

I was impressed watching the women brave the mountain prior to the men's race. One of the men's participants, Steve Carroll, a.k.a. "Crazy Billy," hiked up to the tees and serenaded the women runners as they passed by. "He sang 'Pretty Woman' and some other songs," said Cindy Ruberg of Fairbanks. Another woman said Crazy Billy added an original number about women who run up mountains in Seward.

It started raining shortly before the men's race, so I ducked into a liquor store to take refuge, and suddenly had the urge to buy a few beers and just watch the race from a dry and pleasant spot. The plan was foiled when the proprietor told me I couldn't open beers in the store. I walked outside just as the gun went off and had to run the first fifty yards on the sidewalk. By that time the other runners were at the base of the mountain.

With my competitors out of sight, I had no idea how to approach the mountain, so I started up a rock face. I didn't get far before I was hanging by my fingertips and calling for help. A friendly newspaper photographer advised me to move a few inches to my left. I thanked him and, just as I fell, I heard his camera click.

My legs were bleeding in only a dozen or so places, so I continued up the mountain. Above the cliffs is a scree slope, and to my dismay the race leaders were already loping down this section of the mountain. Scree, by the way, is loose pea gravel. The term derives from the word "screw," which is what a mountain climber says after marching in place for an hour in this gravel. He's out of breath, though, and can't produce the aspirated long "U" sound in "screw." Thus, it sounds like he's saying, "Scree this."

Finally I made it onto hard rock. Seward was far below, the summit far above. A half-hour later I reached the top, utterly exhausted. And naturally, I had to make a decision: I could either slide down the long snow field or run around it.

I'd received mixed advice on this point. Flip Foldager, a Seward resident and Mount Marathon veteran, favored sliding. "You just sit down, yell 'Bonzai!' and go for it," he told me. That sounded better than running, so I took a seat on the snow and prepared to Bonzai! I shoved off and reached warp speed in seconds. By the time I started sliding, you see, the snowfield had been well-greased by the buns of a few hundred kamikaze glissaders, and a chute had formed. So it was basically a luge run minus the luge.

Completely out of control, I shut my eyes and curled into the fetal position. Suddenly I was bouncing over rocks at the bottom of the field, alive if not well. It was the longest and fastest slide I've taken since going from columnist to obituary writer at *The Anchorage Times*.

I began jogging down the mountain with the other laggards. I discovered why the runners taped their socks to their calves when my own socks became filled with rocks on the scree slope. The cliff section was even more challenging on the descent. I thought it best to use the runner in front of me as a human ladder, which for some reason he didn't appreciate. "Scree you!" he shouted as I placed my foot on his shoulder.

The sun was setting when I reached the bottom of the mountain—and remember, this was July in Alaska. All the cheering crowds were gone. I limped along the empty streets toward the finish line.

Rounding the corner downtown, I saw another runner limping along about fifty yards ahead of me. He looked to be in his early 80s. This gave me hope, and I broke into a sprint for the finish line. A few steps from the end, I summoned all my remaining energy and dove headfirst over the line. Those who watched the official Mount Marathon film claim I bowled over the octogenarian, but without a reverse-angle camera they couldn't prove a thing.

Besides, all's fair in love and last place, especially on Mount Marathon.

Later that summer, I went up to Chugach State Park for a hike. As I set out along Powerline Pass, I saw something that stopped me in my tracks: a large red *Anchorage Times* newspaper box. I hate seeing any kind of man-made refuse in a natural setting. But something about the empty box of a deceased newspaper corroding in the wilderness made a powerful — if macabre—artistic statement, and I hoped the box would remain as a kind of tribute.

Way Out There

6

When I told my mother we had a honey bucket, she asked,
"Are the bees much of a nuisance?"

Teaching jobs were hard to come by in Anchorage in the
early '90s. I was also curious about the Alaska Bush and
liked what I heard about the starting salaries, so after
completing my teacher training at UAA, I accepted a job
in Gambell.

Gambell is a Yupik Eskimo village on the northwest tip
of St. Lawrence Island, which is closer to Siberia than main-
land Alaska. The International Date Line hangs a left to avoid
the island, and some days, when the cold and isolation became too much, I wished I had been as wise.

Amy was not thrilled to be leaving Anchorage; she enjoyed her job as a costumer for the opera, not to mention the
trappings of civilization. Still, she gamely decided to give it
a go, and we flew to Gambell in mid-August with our beloved dog, Ilie, and our evil cat, Ziegert.

Our reception was less than warm. Some kids decided to
throw rocks at our house on a regular basis, just for fun; I
think they enjoyed being chased by me. The same culprits
who threw rocks would often drop by later in the day, in-
nocent smiles of their faces, and inquire, "Can we visit?"

I knew the high school principal in Gambell, Andy Haviland, from a summer class at UAA. Andy was a jack-of-all-trades with a fine sense of humor and a talent for putting people at ease. In addition to his duties as principal, he taught a shop class, refereed basketball games, maintained the teacher housing, and filled in when needed as school cook and custodian.

Some years before, Andy had ventured out with some walrus hunters, and they became lost in a heavy fog on the Bering Sea. The hunters ran out of gas and food, and Andy, convinced that death was close, carved a farewell message to his family on his wallet.

Junior Slwooko took charge and kept the hunters optimistic. They used their coats as sails and managed to make it back to an uninhabited part of St. Lawrence Island. From there, they managed to rig a radio and call for help; they were rescued after several weeks and many lost pounds.

The ordeal seemed to instill Andy with a survivor's confidence; he knew the problems that stress most of us were nothing to worry about, when you considered the bigger picture – namely, that you could be cold, wet, hungry and using your coat as a sail.

One of our first adjustments to Gambell concerned waste disposal. A small percentage of the homes in Gambell had running water at the time and thus flush toilets. The rest of the village made do (so to speak) with honey buckets.

Many fortunate folks from Outside are not familiar with honey buckets. When I told my mother in Iowa that we had a honey bucket, she said, "Isn't that charming. Are the bees much of a nuisance?"

CHAPTER SIX

Honey buckets, at least in Alaska, do not hold honey. A honey bucket is a foot-high pail lined with a plastic bag. A child-size seat and lid are attached to the rim.

Situating my six-foot-three frame on the little bucket o' joy was a challenge at first, but I soon mastered the technique – save for those groggy 3 a.m. visits, when my form suffered and I had a tendency to fall overboard.

My initial impulse was to put the honey bucket in the bathroom, where it belonged, by God, even if I had to brush my teeth while holding my nose. Our neighbors, Pete and Beth Sutch, explained that it's best to put the bucket in the Arctic entry, as the cold cuts down on the smell.

The cold also altered my personal habits. For the first time in my adult life I didn't bring reading material along when I was anticipating a sit-down visit. Nor did I linger. Some habits die hard, however, and I still found myself reaching over my shoulder to flush the honey bucket. There should be a psychological term for this tendency.

Air Flush, perhaps.

We installed a curtain in front of the honey bucket area, primarily because we kept Ilie chained at the other end of the entry. Ilie is a huge and hairy mutt-wolf. She has a quizzical stare. The combination made bucket-related functions disconcerting and, at times, downright difficult.

Even with the curtain, our "bathroom" was rustic. And not always private. We learned that no one in Gambell considers Arctic entryways true front doors; if the door was unlocked, they'd walk right in.

I forgot to lock the outer door a few times during early honey bucket sit-downs; twice I had unwelcome visitors. Once I kept very quiet and thought of witty one-liners and hoped the visitor didn't see my sneakers beneath the curtain. The other time I was more bold.

"Hey you," I yelled, "get the hell outta here!"

"Oh, sorry," a man's voice replied, and he beat a hasty exit.

A few minutes later, as I was explaining the untimely visit to Amy, someone knocked on the door. Same guy.

"Would you like to buy some ivory carvings – now?" he asked. Even St. Lawrence Island has pushy salesmen.

We adjusted to the bucket life as well as can be expected, but some newcomers did not. Kris Lucas, another first-year teacher, had a terrible time with her honey bucket at first, mainly because it didn't have a handle. The locals were greatly amused to see her hauling her bucket to the dump like a load of laundry; she clutched it to her chest and, for obvious reasons, threw her head back.

While Kris was suffering this indignity, her husband, Luke, was back home in Wisconsin tidying up details for his own move to Gambell. Kris decided not to tell Luke about the crippled honey bucket. In fact, she thought it would be a wise marital strategy not to mention the honey bucket at all until he set foot on the island.

Needless to say, Luke was surprised by the local plumbing. But he adjusted quickly. He had to, as he was put in charge of the honey bucket detail.

Hauling heavy buckets over soft gravel is a fine workout, although not as much fun as, say, Tae Bo. So we were appreciative when Andy decided to loan us the school fourwheeler once a week for honey bucket runs.

The honey bucket dump was a foul sight – not to mention smell – however you got there. Still, it was more tolerable on a weekly basis. We designated Thursday as Honey Bucket Day and fell into a resigned pattern.

Soon, the pattern did not include our wives. Amy and Kris are independent and capable women, but their feminist attitudes were conspicuously absent on Honey Bucket Day, when they assumed traditional roles faster than you can say Barbara and Laura Bush. In short, they cooked dinner while we hauled buckets.

Luke and I became fast friends – partly, I'm sure, because we shared this distasteful chore. It's impossible to put on airs or be standoffish when you tiptoe through a honey bucket dump with someone. As far as male-bonding activities, it ranks right up there with watching pro football.

Occasionally we got into heavy discussions during our dump run. Once we debated the etymology of "honey bucket." Luke surmised that the phrase entered the language as an ironic term, like Peacekeeper Missile or Rap Music. My guess was that it was a shortened form of a longer expression. This first came to mind in the pre-four-wheeler stage, when Amy would say, all too often, "Honey, go dump the bucket!"

Hence, honey bucket.

7

The wave crashed and took me down, rolling me over several times.

I was designated the boys' basketball coach at Gambell High School, and was looking forward to the season. I saw the boys shooting baskets during lunch, and they had some raw talent, some decent form. The average height was about five-foot-six, but a few could really sky. Too many slung the ball instead of shooting. And they all favored playing at the nine-foot basket.

The school nickname was great: *Qughsatkut*, or "King Polar Bear." That just puts to shame all those Eagles and Rams and such. What's tougher than a King Polar Bear?

I met with the boys interested in playing. I was encouraged to see a dozen show up. I typed up a list of things they would have to do to stay eligible—come to school, pass their classes with a "C" average, don't smoke—and a list of things they would receive. The latter included the opportunity to proudly represent the school and village, and more tangible things such as travel to other villages and letterman jackets. Finally I told them my basketball philosophy, which is simple: run-and-gun offense, pressing defense and using many players.

I was encouraged that all the boys seemed enthusiastic and eager for the season to start. Later that day, I went over to borrow some butter from Pete and Beth. Pete answered the door.

"I hear you're going to be the basketball coach," he said.

"That's right."

"I coached them last year for a couple of weeks," he said. "Until they folded."

"That's what I heard."

"Well, I just have one thing to say." I waited for the inevitable, unwanted advice, but he didn't offer any. He merely made the sign of the cross in front of my face and said, "Bless you, my son."

A couple of days later I glanced out the window between second and third periods and saw almost every boy who attended the basketball meeting smoking. Nearly all the students had a nicotine habit, but I thought some of the jocks might refrain. This was not a good sign.

I found out that Yami was by far the best player in the school. He was only about five-foot-four, but he was a great shooter and passer, and he drove to the basket like a kid going to spend his permanent fund dividend check – fast, fearless and somewhat reckless.

Yami was also a fine student and just a nice kid. In idle moments I considered how easy my job as a teacher and coach would be with a school full of Yamis.

So many of the other students had such serious family problems that school and sports were not a priority. Of course school and sports could help them, if only by providing an escape for a few hours a day. This message was a tough sell.

We had excellent attendance the first two weeks of school, but it fell off, particularly among the boys planning to play basketball. Ben missed a week straight. His grandmother, who works at the school, said he was hunting. When I told Andy this, he laughed and said most of Ben's hunting takes place in front of the television.

My revised goal was to have enough players to compete.

Another potential player, Reggie, was a fiery kid who showed great potential as a rebounder and on defense. More important, he was at school every day. I thought I could count on him all season.

The problem was that Reggie also had a fiery temper. In class I had to constantly remind him not to hit or cuss at his classmates. It got to the point that if he merely pushed someone or muttered an expletive under his breath, I thought, *Well, that's not too bad for Reggie*, and let it pass.

Occasionally Reggie directed his anger towards me; twice he offered to beat me up. I reminded him that if he decked the basketball coach, his playing time would probably suffer.

"We ain't gonna have a team," he said after one such encounter. I was hoping this was not a self-fulfilling prophecy.

During gym classes, Kevin, another reliable student, jumped up to grab the rim. He hung there by one arm, doing a gorilla imitation, then dropped to the floor in pain. His shoulder hurt him for the rest of the day and he had to be flown to Nome for treatment.

Charles was the next casualty; he didn't show up for classes all week, and word was that he stole someone's homebrew and was afraid to leave his house. The diagnosis from Nome, meanwhile, was that Kevin had a separated shoulder and could not play for a few weeks.

When he returned, I had the following conversation with him:

"How's the shoulder?"

"I quit."

"You can't quit what you haven't joined."

"I quit."

"The basketball season hasn't even started!" I said. "I know your shoulder hurts, but it'll heal and you can come out for the team then."

"I quit."

He quit. George, another potential player, had hepatitis. Charles was still in hiding, and Ben was still hunting.

We received some bad news from Nome soon after regarding Kelly, who was there for two weeks on a work-study program. Kelley apparently sneaked into the Unalakleet gym, located a mini-trampoline, and proceeded to soar for slam dunks. On one of his monster jams he came down wrong and blew out his knee.

Someone, I thought, should have been supervising. Unalakleet should have to give us their best student-athlete as compensation. A player to be named later? A draft pick? Anyone?

At the end of the September, I wrote a memo to Andy: "As you know, we're rapidly running out of basketball players. So I was wondering if we could pitch the following idea to the school district: In the event we only have three or four eligible players, we'll use eighth graders for the balance of our team. We'll forfeit the games, but play the other teams in the district anyway. This will give the eighth graders valuable experience (and help the program in the future), provide the fans with a contest to watch (even if it goes in the books as a forfeit), and let the schools make some gate and concessions money. What do you think?"

The memo back said, "John, this will never fly."

Fourteen players turned out for the girls basketball team. I had six boys the first day, enough for doubles tennis the second. I was also less than impressed with their shots; some threw more knuckleballs than a baseball team. At the end of practice they hit a combined 26 for 100 from the free throw line. Lord knows how they would shoot when someone was covering them. I could lock them in the gym all night and they'd probably emerge scoreless the next morning.

Enough! I told myself to be positive, look on the bright side, and hope for a six-two transfer student with a jump shot.

After the third practice, I saw two other boys, Rudy and Brian, sitting in the bleachers. Both were decent students and would be eligible all year. Trying to hide my desperation, I asked if they'd like to practice. Brian shook his head and left. Rudy gave me his squinty, ear-to-ear smile – which I'm sure he'd used to charm people from an early age – and said he'd practice if I paid him five bucks.

The sad part was, I actually considered it. What's five bucks after all?

That's probably how it starts. Then in fifteen years you're a bag man for the booster club, bribing professors for grades, and convincing car dealers that your All-American center really needs a free Lexus.

"Forget it," I told Rudy.

"No pay, no practice," he replied, and left the gym.

Only four players showed up for the last practice of the first week. Sad. Two eighth graders, a seventh grader and Hunter Ben, who was ineligible already. Even lay-up drills are tough with four players. I was on the verge of throwing in the towel.

Rumors of the demise of the boys' basketball team spread quickly through the village. Basketball was the primary means of entertainment and community interaction on weekends, so there was genuine distress. Asked about the situation in my reading class, I told the students that we'd hold practice for a few more days, but that it didn't look good. Angela shook her head in disgust. "We have the dumbest boys in the district," she said to general laughter.

By October of that first year, we were feeling fairly comfortable in Gambell. Amy and I enjoyed bundling up and taking long walks along the mile-long runway, up the bluff, or along the beaches.

We were walking Ilie along the beach one a blustery Sunday afternoon, when we had an experience that would alter our perception of our new home. We'd gone several miles and were near the northwest point when I decided to move down the sloping beach, closer to the water. I threw some rocks, took a few steps along the shore, and saw a shadow out of the corner of my eye.

The shadow was a rogue wave, big as a house and moving fast. I began sprinting up the slope of the beach but the soft gravel hindered my efforts. The wave crashed and took me down, rolling me over several times. I came up for air and was waist-deep in the frigid water, which began receding. I tried to fight the ebbing force, and finally went down on all fours and clawed in the gravel for purchase. Amy, meanwhile, was running through the quickly receding water toward me; she grabbed my jacket hood and helped keep me on shore.

We walked quickly back to our house; I tried to run but my sodden clothes weighed me down. By the time I stripped off my clothes—a few hundred pebbles pattered the floor in the process—I was getting hypothermic. I shivered under blankets for an hour, drank cup after cup of hot tea, and promised Amy I'd be more careful on future walks.

8

You can tell when someone is cussing you no
matter what language.

There were many dangers on St. Lawrence Island. Even
the residents sometimes underrated — or ignored — the power
of nature. One man did so in the fall of our first year on the
island, and paid the ultimate price.

The incident started following a basketball game on a
Sunday night. I was refereeing the game with Andy
Haviland. The contest went into double-overtime, and
Andy and I, having officiated a couple of earlier games
as well, were worn out.

"If it looks like it's going into triple overtime," Andy said
with a wink during a timeout, "I'm taking matters into my
own hands."

On the ensuing play, I called a foul on a village player.
He disagreed strongly with the call and got in my face – and
I got an unwelcome whiff of the whisky on his breath. I
thought he was playing surprisingly well considering he was
under the influence. He continued shouting at me in Yupik,
and although I didn't understand but a few words of the
language, you can tell when someone is cussing you in any
tongue. So I called a technical foul.

As a player from the opposing team was shooting the "T," Andy whispered, "You know you just teed-up an ex-con with a mean streak, right John?"

I hadn't. And at the time I didn't worry much.

Two days later, my brightest and best-behaved student — the ex-con's daughter — arrived in class and began to direct uncharacteristically angry words at me and her classmates; I was on the verge of kicking her out but managed to get her settled down and writing in her journal.

When we moved on to another exercise, she continued writing. The nice thing about dealing with only ten or so students in a class is that you can be more attentive to student moods and work with them individually. I let her continue writing rather than risk another blowup.

By lunchtime we'd heard the news: following the basketball game Sunday night, her father drank some more, become abusive to his family, and took off on his snowmachine — presumably for his fish camp about ten miles away. A friend had gone looking but couldn't find him, so now a search was underway.

That afternoon Hugo Apatiki, the school's custodian and a village leader, sat down next to me in my class and pulled off some of his heavy winter gear; the missing man was his cousin, and he'd been searching for him all day. "I'm worried about that young man," he said.

Hugo left to resume his search, and I read what the missing villager's daughter wrote in her journal. She titled the entry "Fathers," and it told of his struggles. He'd been in prison in Palmer most of the last five years, she wrote; the family visited him on the Fourth of July and had a wonderful picnic, and he promised to get counseling and be a different man when he was freed.

He kept his promise, she wrote—for a while. He received counseling and was clean and sober when he returned to Gambell. And he encouraged his friends to follow his example.

It worked the other way around, his daughter wrote; he began drinking and smoking weed, and became abusive to his family once again.

I finished reading and walked through the gym; the news had spread and several students were in the bleachers, quietly weeping.

Hugo, meanwhile, had found his cousin's snowmachine track. His cousin had travelled south across Troutman Lake, which borders the village and runs parallel to a high bluff. The bluff levels off at the far end of the lake, about two miles distant, and the villager had turned northeast at that point. His snowmachine broke down in deep snow about a mile later; Hugo found tools scattered around the machine and half a bottle of Jack Daniel's in the storage compartment.

Nearby, Hugo saw his cousin's faint footprints. He followed them slowly back down the bluff and onto the lake. His cousin had made a beeline for his house.

But it was moderately cold that Sunday night, about seventeen degrees, and a northerly wind was blowing at 10 mph. He would have been walking into the teeth of the wind across the exposed lake.

His body was about twenty yards from where his footprints ended; he'd dragged himself the final yards on his elbows. Hugo said he was wearing only a light sweatshirt, sweatpants and sneakers.

Following a memorial service, his coffin was taken to the village cemetery atop the bluff, about nine hundred feet above the village. Boulders dot the landscape there, and smaller ones are sometimes used as headstones. The place has the haunting appearance of Stonehenge.

The following Sunday, Jerome dedicated the basketball game to his friend. Jerome's a fine player, but he played with an uncommon intensity that night, scoring on jumpers from all over the court and slashing drives to the basket. I was playing rather than refereeing this game, and neither I nor my teammates could stop him; they won the game and Jerome finished with thirty-eight points — and a fitting tribute to his fallen friend.

In time, I developed an admiration for the essential toughness of the people in Gambell. They generally ignored the dangers of their ancestral island, and went about their lives with a kind of casual courage.

Among the dangers they took for granted were polar bears, which concerned newcomers such as myself. The bear talk started in earnest in early December, when the north wind turned frigid and ice encircled the island. I was curious about the magnificent animals and asked my students many questions. They indulged my curiosity for the most part, but turned it against me when I gave them a writing assignment they disliked.

"Polar bear is gonna get you," Douglas warned.

"King Bear will jump out and assassinate you," added Kelly, who watched too many JFK specials in November.

I dismissed this as the talk of students trying to frighten a naive new teacher. I've hiked and camped in bear country in other parts of Alaska and haven't been worried. Most of the time.

Occasionally, for whatever reason, my imagination will shift gears. Then every sound is a grizzly on the rampage, every movement a psychotic black bear. At such times I've found it helps to sing Bruce Springsteen songs at high volume. "Born to Run" is a favorite.

For almost four months on the island, I had nothing to worry about, save for the odd four-wheeler without headlights flying past me in the dark. That rough sense of security changed in mid-December, when the days grew dark and the first polar bear was spotted near the village.

9

"I jumped on the bear's back and rode him across the lake like Davy Crockett."

Every weekday morning at six-thirty, I walked the half-mile from my house to the high school on the east end of the village. Most mornings I was too groggy to be thinking about bears. But one particular morning seemed ominous.

Snow was blowing horizontally and I could only see about ten feet in front of me. Dawn wouldn't arrive until one in the afternoon, so it was essentially the middle of the night. My goggles were fogging, and I had an uncanny feeling that a polar bear was stalking me—the Freddy Krueger of polar bears, poised to pounce with claws slashing and fangs snapping.

Polar bear is gonna get you. King Bear will jump out and assassinate you...

Nearing the school, I jumped an impressive distance off the ground when I saw a polar bear about twenty feet away and moving quickly. A closer look revealed that it was a polar bear hide on a rack, which the wind had momentarily brought to life.

Obviously, I made it to school safely. Later that afternoon, however, when the storm subsided, hunters killed four polar bears close to the village. An old line came to mind: Just because you're paranoid doesn't mean they're not out to get you.

My subsequent morning treks were brisk and comforted by statistics: vehicular accidents, guns and cigarettes claim more lives each day than polar bears do in a decade.

Still, if I had a vehicle I could have driven to school, if I had a gun I could have protected myself, and if I smoked I might not have been such a nervous wreck. Maybe there's something to be said for living dangerously.

I was not the only teacher concerned about polar bears. Some refused to walk alone through the village during the winter months, staying indoors as much as possible.

By contrast, the Natives didn't seem to fear the bears at all. Patrick Apatiki, an eighth-grader at the time, killed a polar bear while hunting with his father and sister. They spotted tracks near the village, followed the bear south for about twelve miles, and Patrick killed it with a single shot to the neck.

"It was a big bear," he said proudly. "Nine feet long."

Was he scared while hunting such a large animal?

"Nah, it was fun."

Over Christmas vacation, it became apparent that an unusually large number of bears were crossing the ice to St. Lawrence Island that year. In early January, Junior Slwooko and his son Quinn shot seven bears on one hunting trip, and the total kill approached twenty.

In early January, word reached Gambell High School that three polar bears were nearby. The news electrified the students. It was a Friday and teacher Steve Klein immediately took his biology class for the field trip.

I was teaching a computer keyboarding class — typing skills, basically — and would therefore have had more trouble justifying such a field trip. How were polar bears going to enhance typing ability? What's more, it wasn't clear whether the bears were dead or alive.

"Can we go see the polar bears, John?" Charlotte asked.

"Let me think a minute," I said. I thought about my next job interview.

Principal: *Why were you asked to leave your position in Gambell?*

Me: *Two of my students were devoured by polar bears.*

Principal: *I see…*

Me: *But they were typing over forty words a minute before they were, um, consumed…*

It was apparent that the students were not going to stay serenely in class. Sometimes you have flow with the tide of life, and this was clearly one of those times. I cast caution aside and told my class to get their coats. In truth, I wanted to see the bears myself.

We took a shortcut south across Troutman Lake. It was a clear day and the low sun cast a shaky orange path across the ice. We ran and slid toward the sun for a quarter-mile while four-wheelers and snowmachines carrying armed men passed us. Candace interpreted this the same way I did. "They're killing our school mascot!" she said, and picked up the pace.

The bears were indeed dead when we arrived at the scene, shot by Simeon Oittillian as they emerged from a den on the bluff. They were dragged down and set on their backs with their hind legs spread wide and their forelegs curiously upright, like begging dogs. Several men took out knives and began removing the hides while students watched.

CHAPTER NINE

The den was about two hundred feet up the bluff. I went for a closer look. Bright red blood was splattered across the snow at the entrance. The den was about eight feet wide, three feet high and ten feet deep. A safe place, for a time.

The hides and carcasses were loaded and taken back to Gambell. The villagers worked on them all night, cleaning and carving. Much of the meat was eaten and the yellow-white fur appeared as ruffs on parkas and in artwork.

The next morning, I came across Hugo Apatiki cleaning a polar bear skin in a wash basin. I assumed it was one of the bears shot the day before, but Hugo said it wasn't.

"This bear was outside my house this morning," he said. "I jumped on his back and rode him across the lake like Davy Crockett. Then I took out my knife and, one stab, killed him."

It was comforting to know I wasn't the only one with a vivid imagination.

10

I watched the devil beast careen blindly around the room with the carton stuck on his head.

My first teaching experience was enriched by the social gatherings of teachers. We'd play board games and talk shop, gossip, vent our frustrations and cook creative meals. It reminded me of the camaraderie that developed among some of *The Anchorage Times* staffers, sans alcohol.

While I found Gambell challenging and fascinating, Amy had a bleaker outlook. She'd grown up in Anchorage and was content to stay there; we also talked about moving to the Seattle area, which we'd visited on a vacation and found to our liking.

During the day, when I was teaching, Amy tried to occupy herself with her artwork. She is very talented in several disciplines, and we thought she'd have time to focus on some large projects in Gambell. We were pleased to learn that Gambell is home to many gifted artists—carvings from St. Lawrence Island sell for high prices in Aspen, New York and elsewhere around the U.S. Still, it wasn't the traditional, supportive artistic community in which Amy would have thrived.

Amy got along well with Beth Sutch, Kris Lucas and the other teachers, but sometimes, as a non-teacher, she felt excluded from conversations and social gatherings. It didn't help, of course, that I was less than thrilled with the institution of marriage. There is no graceful way to explain to your wife that while you are very fond of her, you'd rather not be married because it infringes on your freedom to hit the road, your periodic need for solitude, and the very occasional opportunities you have to sleep with other women.

Naturally, I kept these thoughts to myself. And naturally, Amy sensed that I was growing restless. One weekend the waves began crashing.

"You haven't told me you loved me a long time," she said.

I hesitated, then said, "I'm not sure I do."

Amy cried, as might be expected, and snapped at me when I tried to comfort her. So I put on my coat and went for a long walk on the beach, thinking about the latest mess I'd made of my life. After about three miles I turned and saw Amy and Ilie trailing after me. I waited, leaning against a boulder near the base of the bluff that backs the village.

We talked much of it out. Amy, good soul that she is, wanted above all to have a strong marriage. "My parents always told me that their marriage works because they both try to do more than their fair share," she said. "Let's both try to do more, honey. I don't want to end up a divorce statistic."

I tried to be a better, more committed husband, and for a time I succeeded. We had a nice holiday season together. In January, however, I became busy with school and often was expected to referee basketball games on weekends; this cut into our time together. Amy was too often by herself during the cold dark days, and she became depressed. She was not alone—another teacher left unannounced on a plane and faxed in her resignation from Arizona.

We agreed that it would be best if Amy took a couple of months off from Gambell. The Anchorage Opera had a show coming up, and she could work, make some money, see her family and friends, enjoy a few restaurants and other urban pleasures.

I took care of Ilie and the evil cat Ziegert while Amy was gone. Amy was the only human in the world who could pet Ziegert without being clawed. I found this out the hard way during our courtship, and after my hands were covered with bloody lines, I gave up trying to be friends. My hands-off policy toward the cat became downright hatred one evening when Amy was sick in bed. I brought her some soup, and we were talking when Ziegert, hidden under the bed, flicked out a paw and clawed the top of my bare foot. I hopped around cussing and threatened to throw the damn cat in a dumpster.

Amy loved the ferocious feline, however, so I did not follow through on the threat. But I did have a measure of revenge. As luck would have it, Ziegert shared my fondness for vanilla ice cream, so after I'd finish a pint, I'd place the carton on the carpet so he could lick out the interior. At just the right moment, when he was slurping away, I'd give the the carton a little kick—and smile as I watched the devil beast careen blindly around the room with the pint stuck on his head.

Anyway, a few days after Amy left the village, Ziegert scared the hell out of me by jumping onto my lap. I braced and covered my face, thinking this was a surprise frontal assault—and was shocked when the cat settled himself and began purring.

I thought it might be an aberration, but Ziegert jumped in my lap for affection everyday thereafter until Amy returned. He just purred away contentedly. *Love the one you're with*, he was saying, and I wish I'd been wise enough to understand then what I know now.

Seven planes a day arrived in Gambell when the weather was decent, and villagers were always coming and going. Many had difficulty adjusting to life off the island, especially in cities such as Fairbanks and Anchorage. As one of my basketball acquaintances put it, "There's too many buildings around. I'm in trouble if I can't see the horizon."

Taking planes off St. Lawrence Island during poor weather was always a bit frightening; some crashes had occurred over the years, and the remains of one plane littered the bluff overlooking the village.

Before flights, the pilots always asked the passengers how much they weighed, which was vital information. After one skinny male teacher thought the women erred on the light side, he announced that he weighed "two-fifty" with a straight face. No sense letting vanity interfere with safety, he figured.

Passengers often included itinerant employees of the Bering Strait School District—we joked about the unfortunate abbreviation, B.S. School District—who generally stayed in Gambell for a week or so before moving onto the next village. A particular favorite was Ray Butts, a counselor. He had a marvelous sense of humor, and started off his talks to the kids by making fun of his own name. "I've been called Fat Butt, Cigarette Butt, every kind of butt you can think of," he'd say. We had Ray over to dinner many times, and he was always good company. Ray had the same easygoing, unflap-pable manner as Andy, and one night when I was working late at school, I found out a possible reason why.

I'm not sure what prompted Ray to talk about his time in Vietnam as an Army Ranger, but I'll never forget the sad and distant look in his eyes as he did so. He said he was walking with his squad through the jungle when one of them stepped on a mine. Ray woke up in a hospital a few days later with severe injuries; he'd almost lost his arm in the explosion.

Then someone told him he was the only survivor. "They said I went a little nuts," Ray recalled. "I really don't re-member."

While Ray's and Andy's brushes with death were horri-fying, they both seemed to be better men as a result. It made me wonder whether I should reflect on my own inevitable death more often, rather than avoid thinking about the sub-ject, as most of us do. Maybe we learn best how to live when we look the Grim Reaper straight in the eye.

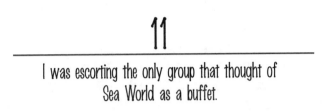

11

I was escorting the only group that thought of Sea World as a buffet.

In the spring, the senior class at Gambell High School headed off on its annual spring trip. My colleague and neighbor, Beth Sutch, developed an ambitious plan—to take the seniors to her home state of Florida for two weeks. Showing the students a completely different world appealed to her, as did the prospect of free housing at the homes of her parents and in-laws.

There were only six seniors in the school—Yami Apatiki, Angela Tungiyan, Brian Aningayou, George Koozaata, Brenda Slwooko and Rudy Oozevaseuk. They worked hard to raise money for their big trip. In all, they raised about eight thousand and received an additional three thousand in donations.

Initially, Beth was planning to chaperone the trip with her husband, Pete, who taught at the elementary school in Gambell. But the administrators thought this was too much like a vacation for the Sutch family, and they also worried that Pete's second-graders would not fare well in his absence.

Enter your friendly neighborhood English teacher. I was asked to chaperone in Pete's stead, a decision that did not sit well with Beth. We might have had trouble getting along for an extended period even without the resentment factor, as we are very different. I think there are two types of people in the world—those who have bounced a check and those who have not. I belong to the former class, Beth the latter, and we squinted at each other across the Gulf of Fiscal Affairs, unable to ever really connect.

We departed Gambell on a Friday in late April, taking two puddle jumper planes to Nome. From Nome we flew to Anchorage, then to Seattle. During our long layover there we took the kids to a park, where, for the first time in their lives, they climbed trees.

It was touching to see how fascinated the students were by things we take for granted: cars, butterflies and jumbo toilet paper in bathrooms were of particular interest. Television and computers have exposed them to many aspects of life outside the island, but there is no substitute for the rich details of everyday experience. Beth and I discussed the ethics of exposing the students to these wonders, knowing that most of them will never leave the island again. Was the trip a taste of the good life that would turn bitter in years to come? Hard to say, although we concluded that knowledge of the world outside the island might just as easily benefit them.

The next leg of our odyssey took us to Denver; we endured another layover before heading to Kansas City and, finally, Atlanta, which was as far as our discount tickets would take us. We were all sick of planes by the time we reached the continental U.S., and the last legs were the worst.

I slept fitfully and kept jolting awake to find that I was drooling on my shirt. This, however, did not discourage a woman in the next seat from striking up a conversation with me concerning the "Mexican kids" who called to me from time to time, usually in regard to how long they would be stuck on the plane.

I explained that they were Yupik Eskimos, not Mexicans. This piqued her curiosity and she asked the dreaded igloo question. I explained that while they might build an igloo if they were caught in a storm, Eskimos do not live in them full-time. Why would they? Cold, damp, dark, no cable TV — igloos suck.

"Like, do they have a mall out there?" she asked.

"No," I said, "there's just a general store."

"That's where they shop for food?"

"Some of it. They also hunt."

"For what?"

"Whales, seals, walrus, polar bears, birds — whatever they can get."

"That's sick."

"Well, they've been hunting those animals for hundreds of years, and they'd have starved without them. So you really shouldn't judge them." This reproach thankfully ended our conversation, and I returned to napping and drooling.

We stayed over with some of Beth's relatives in Atlanta, then drove our fifteen-passenger van to Largo the next day. The first conflict between Beth and me arose on the drive, a foreshadowing of things to come. During a rest stop, I threw out a bag of garbage in the back seat. Shortly thereafter George became hungry and started looking around for the chips.

"They were in a bag back here," Beth said. "Where did it go?"

"I threw out a bag of garbage," I said.

"It looked like garbage, but there was food in there, too."

"Usually it's a good idea to keep the food separate from the garbage," I noted. We didn't speak for about one hundred miles, whereupon we returned to being civil with one another.

We reached Largo at midnight. All the kids immediately jumped in the pool. Only two could swim so we corralled the others in the shallow end. I stayed with the boys at the home of Beth's parents, Edward and Renee Johnson, while she stayed with the girls at her in-laws, Frank and Ruth Sutch. Both families were warm and hospitable.

The next day we had lunch with some friends of the Johnsons. They took us to Columbia's, a fine Cuban restaurant on Sand Key. I was seated at one end of a long table, next to Brenda and across from a woman with a heavy southern accent.

During the meal, Brenda asked why I put my napkin on my lap. I explained that it was considered polite manners and also came in handy catching any food that might drop off the plate. At this point the woman across the table looked me straight in the eye and said: "You peed on the floor."

"No, Ma'am, I didn't," I said.

"You peed on the floor," she repeated, louder still and so matter of factly that I thought she must be right. Drooling on my shirt, peeing on the floor — I was becoming a social embarrassment. I looked under the table and realized that while in Gambell I'd lost my ability to decipher accents. The woman was commenting on my napkin-catching theory, I realized, and in a sense she was right: My pea was indeed on the floor.

Later that day, while Beth was besieged with relatives, I took the seniors on a nature walk around a nearby lake. We were startled by the lush greenery and abundance of animals, including egrets and pair of alligators. A bird made a high pitched caw-caw noise that was familiar to Angela. "Sounds like my grandma when she's pissed off," she said.

Brian, meanwhile, looked like a boxer as he ducked and bobbed to avoid the lovebugs and dragonflies. The natives in Gambell hunt one-hundred-ton whales in skin boats, chase polar bears across shifting sea ice and demonstrate their courage in many other ways, but they have a genuine fear of insects. This probably stems from the time when missionaries told them that bugs spread disease and death. In any case, I have seen a fly cause a fire drill at the high school, and the abundance of bugs in Florida had the seniors spooked, despite our assurances.

The next day I took the boys to the beach at Sand Key while Beth took the girls shopping for bathing suits. The guys, of course, were impressed with the bikini-clad women parading along and even made some half-hearted passes. They might have been the first Eskimos in history to hit on Florida women.

Rudy, Brian and George asked if they could go buy sodas and, after pointing out some landmarks to assure their safe return, I told them to go ahead. My priority was the remaining student who could drown in the Gulf of Mexico.

Rudy returned about fifteen minutes later. After a half-hour, I began to worry a bit about Brian and George, and asked Rudy where they went.

"I'm not going to tell you," he said, flashing his charming, squinty-eyed smile. I pressed Rudy until he confessed that they'd gone to a tattoo parlor. We packed up and went after them but arrived as they were walking out with bandages on their shoulders. George's bandage covered a heart-shaped American flag, Brian's a heart bearing the names of his girlfriend and son.

We talked. They told me they lied because they were afraid I would have told them they couldn't get tattoos. I said I didn't think it was a great idea, but they were young adults, I was treating them as such, and within the established rules, they could do what they wanted. I felt a new level of trust and mutual respect taking hold after that discussion.

We spent an enjoyable day at Cypress Gardens, during which Beth confessed a secret desire to join the Aqua Maids and George's outgoing personality flourished during the first of several media interviews. The reporters all wanted to know how Eskimos were handling the Florida sun, and Rudy summed it up best when he said they were "humongous hot." Still, they all tanned well, unlike me.

"John, how come you just turn a little red?" George asked. "Too many white blood cells?"

"That must be it, George."

Toward the end of the first week, we took them to Largo High School, Beth's alma mater, where they each shadowed a senior for a day. They were intimidated going into a school of two thousand students. "I think I'm gonna cry," Brenda said. But the Largo students were friendly and politely inquisitive.

An awkward moment occurred when the Largo kids asked the Gambell seniors if they had any questions. Our students shook their heads, which some of our hosts found rude. A possible reason was that Yupik Eskimos tend to learn more by observation and experience, rather than questions or trial and error. The Yupiks watch closely and loathe mistakes. A mistake on St. Lawrence Island—getting too close to a polar bear, for example, or taking the wrong path among the ice floes – can prove fatal.

We spent most evenings watching cheap movies, eating fast food, playing miniature golf and driving around Clearwater listening to Bubba the Love Sponge on the radio. One night, heading out to eat, Beth was driving and turned her head to ask a question. Suddenly a car ran a stop sign and was directly in front of the van, and we were about to T-bone it. "Jesus Christ!" I yelled and braced for impact. With admirable quickness, Beth jerked the wheel, and we squealed around the back of the car, missing by perhaps a foot. A shocked silence ensued, followed by everyone talking at once. "My mouth fell open," Angela said. "My eyes got real big," George said. "Let's do it again," Brian added. Beth credited her guardian angel with saving us while I took the Lord's name in vain a few more times. We'd been lucky.

On Friday of that first week, Beth had a dentist's appointment, and I took the students to Tarpon Springs to see some family friends, Dave and Judy Murphy. We spent the afternoon swimming, exercising in the Murphy's garage gym, and eating a spread that would have fed all of Largo High. I was proud that the students were so polite.

Afterward, I took them to Countryside Mall. We'd been there before, and once again I told them to meet at the ice rink in the middle of the mall at 6:30 p.m. At the designated hour, five of the six seniors were there. Yami, the most reliable of the bunch, was missing. After waiting twenty minutes, I began to worry. He was not the type of kid to be late unless there was a real problem. So I contacted mall security, and we began hunting for him. I walked from one end of the mall to the other several times, checking stores that might appeal to him as I went. I don't have any children myself, but I began to appreciate those worry lines I've seen etched in the faces of many parents.

Finally, just as Angela was beginning to cry, Yami showed up. He said he was sleepy and didn't hear when I gave instructions on the meeting point and time. So he'd wandered around the parking lot looking for the van. I was so relieved he was back that I didn't even get mad.

The following day we met with Mark Tobin, a former teacher in Gambell, and went canoeing down the Withlacoochee River. The river was low, but all the talk of alligators and snakes motivated several of us who capsized on the rocks to right ourselves quickly.

Back in Largo on Sunday, some of us walked across the street to attend Mass at St. Patrick's Church. Boy Scouts were outside the church selling raffle tickets. Shortly after Mass began, two uniformed police officers walked up the center aisle, looking this way and that. They found the man they were looking for and escorted him outside. I half expected the guy to hunch over and shout, "Sanctuary! Sanctuary!" But he went peacefully enough. Later, I learned that he'd tried to sell crack to the Boy Scouts.

Alaska can be an odd place, but it has nothing on Florida.

Early on Monday, we set off for Orlando. Our first stop was Sea World, and it turned out to be an educational day, with a behind-the-scenes tour that greatly interested the students. They know much about sea life and were anxious to learn more.

They also enjoyed the shows, particularly a slapstick routine starring sea lions. A walrus in a bit part, however, looked unhealthy to their experienced eyes — though not so unhealthy that they wouldn't have enjoyed a slab off his side for dinner. "This is making me hungry for Eskimo food," Brenda said.

I was escorting the only group that thought of Sea World as a buffet.

Shamu, though, was taboo. Pods of orcas sometimes appear off St. Lawrence Island, but the villagers will only hunt bowhead whales. "There's old stories that if you kill an orca, they'll come back and get you," Brian explained. Upon closer inspection, Shamu did seem the vengeful sort.

Of course we went to Disney World, and the students enjoyed all the rides until we reached Splash Mountain and its trademark vertical plunge. Angela was so scared that she tried to crawl under her seat; in the automatic picture taken of each group, all you can see are a few strands of her hair. Rudy didn't especially enjoy the drop either. "Look at me," he said as we exited, "I'm shaking." He swore off roller coasters and other frightening rides then and there.

Beth and I stayed with the students for most of the major attractions. We decided to cut them loose at 4 p.m. and meet at Cinderella's Castle at 6:30 p.m. I followed the plan, but the kids did not. Unbeknownst to me, they'd followed Beth around and wanted to leave early when it started raining. So Beth was angry when she met me, complaining that I'd left her with all the kids. I countered that she'd changed the plan, not me. She said I should have stuck around a few minutes to see where the kids would head. We went back and forth few more times when we returned to our hotel and finally decided not to speak to each other.

Later, the group wanted to go to a nearby Ferris wheel and go-cart track. The silent chaperones grudgingly went along. The kids paired off at the Ferris wheel, leaving Beth and me in the same seat. It was an uncomfortably quiet ride for five seconds, until she broke the ice by saying, "Well, I guess we're stuck with each other."

"Guess so," I agreed.

"This isn't a good place to fight," she added as we reached the apex, and once again I concurred. We were friends again.

The go-carts were the most popular activity among the seniors. They drive Honda four-wheelers in Gambell and go-carts handled in similar fashion. They ignored the "no bumping rule" and tried to run each other off the track.

Afterward, Yami noticed the bungee tower nearby. And his eyes lit up. He declared that he wanted to jump. We talked it over, and concluded that bungee jumping was probably far safer than taking a plane off St. Lawrence Island in poor weather. We let Yami go for it, and I decided to take the leap as well—although, in all honesty, my decision was based more on my own curiosity than going below and beyond the call of duty as a chaperone.

I went first. I was not especially nervous until I looked down from the platform seventy-five feet up. Then I swallowed hard a few times. The New Zealanders at A.J. Hackett Bungy assured me that some fear is normal. So they gave me a countdown from five and when they reached two I learned forward into a swan dive. They didn't quite adjust the length enough to compensate for my weight, and my head scraped the foam pad, but otherwise I enjoyed the experience thoroughly.

Yami's eyes were wide when it was his turn to go, but he dedicated his jump to Gambell and took the dive—more or less. At the last second he figured a jump was wiser and went feet first. The chaperones breathed again when we saw him dangling from the cord and laughing.

The tone was set for the rest of the evening—by far the best of the trip. Angela summed our experiences: "We learned to swim, we saw alligators, we got tattoos, we almost got in a car accident, we went canoeing, we went to Sea World, we went to Disney World, we raced go-carts and we went bungee jumping." Neither Yami nor I minded the all-inclusive pronoun; like the best of teams we had jelled and were working in harmony. We spent several hours driving around and enjoying a rare camaraderie.

Alas, all good things come to an end, and our cohesiveness lasted about two days. Then one of the boys made a feeble attempt to break into a bottle of rum at the Johnson's house, and when Beth and I came down hard on him, we naturally lost some of our group unity.

Our last big event was Busch Gardens in Tampa. I should note here that despite our differences, I admired Beth's intelligence and good heart, and held her in great respect. She simply had a bad day at Busch Gardens. And so did I.

Then there was Rudy, who is not a morning person. I'd had trouble getting him up throughout the trip; generally he'd cuss me while trying to go back to sleep, and the pattern continued when we rose early to go to Busch Gardens. A few hours later when an animal trainer told us that snakes often strike when they are awakened, I teased Rudy that he's the same way.

As the day wore on and the Florida sun bore down, Rudy became aggravated. He was also tired from getting up early and the accumulated effect of two weeks' action. He fell behind the group a few times, and when I encouraged him to keep up, he encouraged me to perform some anatomical impossibilities.

Generally I ignore obscenities; I agree with the late Anthony De Mello's variation on the "I'm Okay, You're Okay" philosophy, which states that "I'm an Ass, You're an Ass." So why get upset when someone inevitably points out the fact? Plus, Gambell is a rough place, and the residents use rough language.

As the day progressed, however, I became increasingly annoyed by Rudy's obstinate and disrespectful behavior. Finally he cussed me one too many times, and I blew up. I got in his face, yelled at him and demanded an apology. He cussed me some more; I said we weren't leaving until he apologized.

We went out to the parking lot when Busch Gardens closed. Angela put her arm around Rudy and they took a walk to cool off. I trailed at a safe distance to make sure they didn't do anything foolish, like run away. When they returned to the van, I reiterated my demand for an apology. None was forthcoming, but I could see that peer pressure and the sun were in my favor and the incident would end soon.

Then Beth contradicted me in front of the kids, saying we had to get going. We strolled away for a pithy conversation, and I was tempted to make some uncharitable remarks. Back at the van, the kids took Beth's lead and started cussing me as well. I told them to be quiet. Rudy threatened to beat me up and added that couldn't touch him or I'd get fired. I said that was true, but if he hit me I was sure as hell going to hit him back. We drove to Largo in the silence that follows a war. I was livid.

The situation was terrible. Right or wrong, I was a white outsider in a native village, and all Rudy had to do was call home and complain to his folks and I'd have to take the next plane out of Gambell. That's the way it is.

At the Sutch residence, Beth surprised me by apologizing in front of the group. She told Rudy he needed to apologize, too. I was still hot and must admit I was pleased when Rudy took the opportunity to cuss out Beth.

While most of us jumped in the pool to cool down, literally and figuratively, Rudy stayed in the van and fumed. He locked himself in his room upstairs a few hours later and didn't even come down for pizza. A definite trouble sign.

As I'd developed an affinity for Florida, I was tempted to start looking through the "help wanted" ads.

The next morning Rudy came downstairs. The smile that gives joy was on his face, and he apologized. We shook hands; I said I was sorry for getting so angry.

We were back on track and the trip ended well. After two weeks in Florida, the kids were ready to return to their island home. They cheered when we set off for the long journey to the world's end.

Sadly, the trip's divisive events and subsequent story I wrote for a magazine ended the friendship Amy and I had developed with Pete and Beth Sutch. They were good and generous neighbors. They were also very adventurous. The summer after they left Gambell, they rode their bicycles from Alaska to Florida, and they spent the next several years pedaling around the rest of the world.

12

It was time to bench Hamlet and bring in Newton.

My second year in Gambell, near the end of a basketball game between a city league team and the school staff, a teacher dove for a loose ball. As he slid across the floor, Allen, a young player on the village team, ran over and drove his knee into the teacher's neck. The teacher was down for several frightening moments. He recuperated but suffered from neck pain for several weeks.

The incident passed, but Allen—who is about six-two and two hundred pounds—seemed to think that it was open season on teachers. He threw elbows and forearms, and some teachers hit the court hard. Several decided not to play basketball anymore for fear they'd be injured or get in a fight.

You think twice about fighting when your adversary is heavily armed when he's not playing basketball, and the nearest cop is two hundred miles away in Nome.

By process of elimination, my teammate, Robert "Luke" Lucas and I were Allen's primary targets. We both enjoyed the game too much to stop playing because a young man was going through a bullying phase. Still, Allen's dirty play began to annoy me. His elbows seemed to have an almost magnetic attraction to my rib cage, and his pushes and shoves could be vicious. He challenged me to fight a few times, an offer I always declined.

His comments made it obvious that he didn't like white people, a sentiment shared by certain others in the village. Some whites who've lived in Gambell a long time said cultural relations had soured in recent years. They said the Yupik community resented the way whites denigrated their culture and made them feel inferior, and now they're standing up for themselves. This sort of cultural pride is healthy, and could help the village in the long run. In the short run, though, life in Gambell was difficult for white teachers such as myself. It's hard to focus on the big picture when a student calls you white trash or a young man aims elbows at your Adam's apple.

The situation was exacerbated by our city league basketball teams, which were competing for bragging rights in the village. Most games between the Hunters (I'm the token non-hunter on the Hunters) and the Phazers were close, and that increased competitive tensions. During a game over the Christmas holiday, when neither Luke nor I were playing, the teams got into an all-Yupik brawl.

For months I tried to ignore Allen's cheap shots and taunts. When things became testy, I'd interject humor, counsel peace, urge restraint and, if all else failed, retreat to the corner for outside shots.

Fear was a factor. I hadn't been in a fight since high school, when I had two. I fractured my left hand in both fights, the second time so badly that to this day I can barely make a fist and the knuckle above my pinkie has all but disappeared. A few years after I effectively lost my hand to battle, I needed oral surgery to close a gap between my top and bottom teeth. The doctor broke my jaw in four places and reset it. He told me afterward that the operation was successful, but that it left me with what boxers call a "glass jaw." I've also inherited my father's bad back, which I sometimes throw out and walk around like a hunchback for a few days. A fight, I knew, could leave me in that position for weeks.

The summer before, to help keep my back strong and loose, I began studying Tai Chi, the slow, gentle cousin of Karate and Tae Kwon Do. I practiced daily, and my back problems soon disappeared. I also mastered some moves that, as relations deteriorated, I considered using in a fight against Allen.

I could have defended myself with "Sweep Lotus with Leg and Single Whip." I could have attacked with "Shoot the Tiger" and the aptly named "White Snake Puts Out Tongue." And I could have utterly confounded him with "Fair Lady Works the Shuttles."

Of course, it might have been enough to look him in the eye and say in a forbidding tone: "I'm warning you, Allen — I know Tai Chi."

If he went for the bluff, I could have played ball in peace. If he didn't, I'd most likely be a one-handed, glass-jawed guy in deep trouble. Allen, of course, wouldn't be moving at Tai Chi speed — which is only slightly quicker than a beached beluga — and I wasn't sure if I could fast-forward my moves.

The last option I considered was more appealing. I outweighed Allen by about thirty pounds, and, given sufficient cause, I thought I'd introduce him to Newton's Second Law of Motion. This states that Force equals Mass times Acceleration — or, to put it in more basic terms, "Watch out for that truck!"

During our next game, the Phazers fell far behind. Allen grew frustrated. He hit me in the head with an elbow, and I lost my temper. I cursed and threatened him. The presence of my mouth guard made it sound something like this: "Moo Mumuma Mitch! Mime Monna Mick More Mutt!"

It was time to bench Hamlet and bring in Newton. On the next play, when Allen cut through the middle, I took a few quick steps toward him and lowered my shoulder. We collided hard. He fell back and emitted a "whooomf" sound that warmed my heart.

Recovering quickly, he launched a wild swing. I was ready and ducked under it. Players from both teams separated us, and the referee called a technical foul. Afterward, city league officials suspended Allen from the gym for a week.

The next time our teams met was in late February, in the semifinals of the Gambell Shoot-Out. Eleven teams from Gambell and Savoonga participated in the tournament. The winner between the Hunters and Phazers would play Bering Sea, a fine Savoonga team, in the men's final.

The game was close. With two minutes left, the Phazers pulled away to win and advance to the finals. Allen and I exchanged some hard shots during the contest, but nothing cheap.

We gathered for the ritual post-game handshake – which, as coaches know, is always a potentially dangerous time. Then it happened: a spontaneous huddle of both teams, twenty players each extending one arm into the middle, like the spokes of a wheel.

Hands piled up in the center. The pile began lifting and dropping in rhythm as we began chanting, softly at first and then with growing volume: "Gambell, Gambell, GAMBELL, GAMBELL, GAMBELL! It was a display of brotherhood in which there were no Yupiks or whites or teams, just friends playing for the same village and wishing each other well.

Afterward, I had my first pleasant conversation with Allen and some of his teammates. As we talked we realized that in some ways we're not all that different. I didn't know if this feeling of kinship would survive the next game or the next week. I did know I'd never forget that circle of athletes who, for a moment, rose above all differences.

13

"Our uncle caught a whale!"

Most of the high school boys were absent from school the first week in April; this was expected. Whaling season was under way and the ice on the Bering Sea beginning to break. So the boys rose early every morning and gathered their gear. They joined their crews and were on the water by 9 a.m.

In Gambell, whaling is a passion that evokes reverence and joy. The villagers seemed mostly oblivious to the dangers inherent in hunting one-hundred-ton bowhead whales while floating in a boat made of skin. Likewise, shifting ice, frigid waters and long exposure to subzero temperatures are considered part of the game rather than lethal threats.

I didn't hear much about the first hunt of the year until after 9 p.m. one evening, when a man called and immediately began a monologue in Yupik. I interrupted and said he must have the wrong number. He apologized in English, recognized my voice, and identified himself as Tony. We'd become acquainted while playing basketball over the winter.

"I'm in Nome," he said, "and I heard they got a whale."

I hadn't heard and I was two-hundred miles closer to the action. After saying goodbye to Tony, I decided to have a look.

Four-wheelers and snowmachines passed me as I walked to the west beach. It was a fine evening—clear, a relatively warm ten degrees, light breeze. A night without heavy winds in Gambell is about as rare as a night without heavy gunfire in Los Angeles, so a mere breeze was a blessing.

Nearing the elementary school, I was cut off by one of the ubiquitous four-wheelers. Two girls were aboard. "Our uncle caught a whale!" driver Jill Campbell shouted over the engine noise. I hadn't seen her so excited since she pinned a boy in the junior high school wrestling meet.

A familiar voice called my name as I passed through the old village. I didn't see anyone. The voice called again, and looking skyward I saw my friend Hugo Apatiki smiling down from a high window in a dilapidated house, binoculars dangling from his neck. "They got a whale," he said. "They'll probably be back in about two hours."

The beach was crowded with villagers drawn by the news. Everyone seemed to be glowing with excitement. This was Christmas Eve and the Fourth of July all at once—a mystical moment, a magical interlude, as if a spell had been cast.

Some whale hunts are not so peaceful. One time a squall hit as the villagers were hauling a whale to the beach. High waves were crashing into the shore ice, and the men were concerned that the boats would be smashed. They came as close as possible, then threw a rope to a man waiting on shore. A dozen of us then grabbed the rope and ran up the beach, controlling the boat and pulling the whalers to safety.

We'd run a half-dozen boats ashore in this manner when Wilfred Tungiyan fell overboard. Wilfred was weighed down with gear and wasn't much of a swimmer; he might easily have been lost, but he somehow managed to paddle back to his boat. The others on board yanked Wilfred out of the cold water. "I kept picturing my wife and kids, and knew I had to stay alive," he told me later.

When the storm subsided and the whale was cut open, they found a fetus inside. Some thought this was the reason why the dangerous squall occurred.

But this day was different, and seemed blessed rather than cursed. I joined a group standing on the shore. Using a large ice floe as a bearing, Salvador Campbell pointed out the position of the whalers. Through my binoculars I could make out the line of boats and a vague, dark shape beside them. They were about a mile and a half southwest of the village.

I asked Salvador when the strike was made. "I don't know," he said. "I heard about it right after *Rescue 911*."

Slowly the news filtered in via citizens band radios. Keith Oozeva had hurled a harpoon and scored a direct hit, killing the whale even before the explosive head detonated. Alex Oozeva, captain of the boat, was given credit for taking the first whale of the year. "Ta-taa-ta-taa! Aghvenguut!" came the cries over the CBs. We got a whale!

Before the strike, the hunters traveled under traditional sail power so they wouldn't spook the sensitive bowheads. But afterward the other boats opened up their outboard motors and made for the Oozeva boat as quickly as possible. Once there, they roped the boats together and lashed the whale beside them. Then the flotilla, eighteen boats strong, sought a route back to Gambell through the ice floes.

"Those guys are lucky," Salvador said. "They're already eating mangtak. I should have been out there, but I had to do laundry today."

The sun cast pink and blue watercolors across the sky and sea and, over the water in Siberia, tinged the Chukchi Range mountains with alpenglow. In the foreground, children clambered atop house-sized blocks of shore ice.

The April sun lingers past 11 p.m. this far west in the broad Alaska time zone, and it wasn't until midnight that the children's features faded to silhouettes. On shore, clusters of villagers laughed and talked, the deep, consonantal hum of Siberian Yupik carrying a surprising distance. Some speculated whether the whalers would butcher the bowhead on the ice or continue to wait for an opening. "We don't control the ice," Salvador noted.

Many of the male elders and the boys too young to hunt began taking four-wheelers across the ice in the direction of the whalers. They followed a serpentine trail around huge ice blocks while we followed the progress of their flickering headlights. Overhead, the northern lights began to stretch and recoil.

I was always amazed at how the hunters knew what path to take across the ice. A longtime missionary explained it by telling me about the time he invited a villager and his wife to San Francisco for a vacation. When they arrived in the Bay area, the missionary drove through the streets for an hour to his son's house. The villagers, who had not ventured further than Nome previously, were awestruck that he could make sense of all the streets among all the buildings.

Later that year, the missionary asked his friend how he navigated the ice. The Native smiled and said, "It's kind of like San Francisco."

After an hour the four-wheelers returned with some of the young whalers and even a few boats in tow. A woman on a snowmachine, thinking they might have also brought back some of the whale, buzzed toward the new arrivals screaming, "Give me some of that mangtak!"

Shirlene Campbell, a teaching assistant at the high school, asked if I'd ever eaten mangtak, the dark skin and underlying blubber. I replied that I hadn't and asked what it tasted like.

"Just like coconut," she said.

I looked at her and could tell she wasn't pulling the white man's leg, and shook my head with a smile. We research and classify and hypothesize, but can we ever understand a world in which a whale tastes like a coconut?

The whalers spent a cold night with their catch. A path through the ice opened in the wee hours and they had the whale to shore by 6 a.m. Attendance was down again when school opened three hours later; the best education was at the beach anyway, so that's where I took the two girls who came to my first-period class.

It was a small bowhead, about thirty feet long. The whalers had secured it to the shore ice a quarter-mile from the beach. A pink patch about a yard square was carved in the middle of the bowhead's back, revealing where the whalers had snacked during the night.

After working the kinks out of a pulley system, the whalers enlisted the help of some observing teachers in hoisting the whale out of the water. About forty men tugged on the ropes while the women gathered nearby to watch. The Yupik women here govern, run businesses and participate in all aspects of society—with the exception of whaling, which is the province of men.

Once the whale was on the shore ice, Alex Oozeva climbed on its back. He stood literally and figuratively above the rest of the village, proud and happy, and celebrated his triumph with an impromptu Eskimo dance, his hands thrusting outward in time with this bending knees.

He began butchering the whale, cutting horizontal slabs with a hoelike tool. Large hunks would be distributed to virtually everyone in the village. One of the whalers hauling a heavy slab of blubber across the snow turned to look at a teacher videotaping the process and yelled, "Where's the beef?"

By late afternoon the whale's jawbone — the trophy — was pulled up next to the Oozeva boat near the old village. What was left of the carcass was enshrouded in gulls. The beach was empty, the sky filled with slate-gray clouds. Fog was hanging on the bluff, menacing, like the despair that occasionally settles over a village. I walked home fighting a strong north wind and a slight depression.

The spell of the whale was broken.

14

He was hiding, I was plotting.

Near the end of my second year in Gambell, I traveled with the Hunters to Nome to play in the annual basketball tournament that coincides with the running of the Iditarod. We played very well and made the semifinals. Amy remained in Gambell because plane tickets to and from Nome were expensive, and she'd recently returned from a trip to Anchorage.

The basketball was a welcome distraction from the troubles in our relationship. My wanderlust was resurfacing, and I was getting anxious to be out of Gambell—and on my own. When I wasn't playing in a game during the tournament, I often sat in the Nome Public Library, half-reading books and magazines and plotting my escape from the chains of marriage.

One afternoon while I was thus engaged, one of my basketball buddies from the village came into the library and sat in a chair in the corner, hidden from view to anyone near the entrance. Noticing me, he tossed his hand in a little wave; I waved back and asked him what he was doing—he obviously wasn't in the library to read.

"Hiding from my friends," he said. "They want to go to the bars. I'm trying to stop drinking."

He was hiding, I was plotting. Sometimes there is nothing in the world more difficult than being honest with people you care about and should trust.

Back in Gambell, I tried to work up the courage to tell Amy I wanted to separate. We'd been through the tears and anguish caused by my restlessness before, and I simply couldn't endure another round. I half-convinced myself that taking off and sending her a letter would be a bold move into a new life…but I knew the lie and felt like a coward.

She left the village a few days before me, and I sent her the letter. I tried to be sensitive and consoling while making it clear I wanted a final break; it was a painful letter to write, and probably more painful for Amy to read. I went to Seattle and spent a miserable month—my "bold" move offered none of the freedom I'd hoped to find, just guilt and anguish. I thought about returning to Anchorage and humbly asking Amy if we could start fresh, but I didn't. And I've regretted that decision ever since.

Photo Gallery

PHOTOS
(top to bottom, left to right):

First page:
1. Amy
2. Fern and I on O'Malley Peak
3. Fishing on Alexander Creek

Second page:
4. My brother Mike and I on Pioneer Peak.
5. Amy and Ilie
6. Fern and Rod on Patarmigan Peak
7. Snowmachining on Tetlin Lake
8. Kayaking in Halibut Cove

PHOTO GALLERY

PHOTOS
(top to bottom, left to right):

First page:
1. Eskimo dancers
2. Kids in Gambell
3. Target for Tetlin hunters

Second page:
4. Sailing in Seward
5. Ole on a hike.
6. Creek near Tetlin.
7. Gambell seniors in Florida

Coming and Going

15

Proficiency at basketball is the quickest way to winning respect in a Bush village.

After Seattle, I decided to move closer to my family. Most of them had migrated from Chicago to Minneapolis during my years in Alaska. I was going through a divorce and my mother was ailing, so it seemed a good plan.

I stayed for three years in Minneapolis, during which I bored my family, friends and students with tales of The Great White North. I was warned early that Alaska becomes part of your soul, and that I would not fit in well Outside if I left, but I suppose I had to experience this truth for myself.

In 1998, a year after my mother passed away, I left Minnesota in the rearview mirror and drove back to Alaska via New Mexico. The long drive gave me time to sort my thoughts. I'd felt terrible guilt about leaving and subsequently divorcing Amy. I missed her, too, and belatedly realized what a sweet and wonderful soul she was — and just how stupid I was for running off. "Life," wrote John D. MacDonald, "is the process of finding out — too late — everything that should have been obvious in the first place."

I had some unrealistic thoughts of rekindling our relationship, but I'd hurt her too badly and let too much time pass—she'd moved on and wanted nothing to do with me. As for other women, I'd pretty much gone 0-for-Minnesota. And while the odds were not as good in Alaska, I tended to get along better with Alaska women than those Outside, so I was hopeful that I'd meet someone.

I stopped for lunch in Tok my first day back in Alaska. I felt out of place, and then realized it was because I was the only man in the restaurant without a beard.

Not many guys wore beards in Minnesota – at least not real beards. Sure, there were guys with the half-committed mustache, the pretentious stubble, the satanic goatee, and the patch of hair that dangles from the lower lip like a forgotten piece of pasta. None of that nonsense is found in the true north. No, Alaskans don the Full Castro.

In some ways the beard is a symbol of Last Frontier men: tough, rugged, pragmatic. And Alaska women—unlike those Outside—do not seem to mind going through the woods to get to the picnic. I soon grew my beard back—although it was a while, I must admit, before I enticed any picnickers to pucker through my particular woods.

While eating at Fast Eddy's, I saw a few small buildings across the road with a sign that said, "Alaska Gateway School District." I was in need of a job, so I thought I'd drop in and see if they had any available.

As it turned out, there was an opening for a principal-teacher in Tetlin, an Athabascan Indian village about twenty-five miles southeast of Tok. I was flown in to Tetlin that same afternoon for an interview with the school board.

The board members asked a few polite questions about my experience. Then Bernie Paul, the head of the board and the village's cop, asked me to step into the gym. We shot baskets for about ten minutes and Bernie was pleased to see that I could play the game. "You have a good jumper," he said. "Lot better than the old principal. You got the job."

I'd forgotten that proficiency at basketball is the quickest way to winning respect in a Bush village. I suppose this unusual hiring should have warned me about the village's priorities. Still, it was a relief to have a job relatively early the summer.

16

If you can't tie a knot, tie a lot.

With some free time, I went down to Seward, one of my favorite places in the state, and took a week-long sailing class with seven other enthusiasts. We all had our reasons for taking the course. Peggy Dunwoodie was heading to Florida to buy a live-aboard sailboat in the 32- to 36-foot range. Dave and Karen Summerfeldt were thinking about buying a sailboat, as were Doug and Milisa Zornes. And brothers Paul and Mark Stearns were planning to charter a boat with family members in the Greek Isles.

As for me, I knew the basics of sailing small boats, but was interested in learning how to handle the larger ones. I thought it would be nice to buy – or at least be able to charter – a boat big enough to accommodate friends and family members. I also thought it would be nice to return friends and family members to shore without any water in their lungs.

We spent the first three days splitting our time between the boats in Resurrection Bay and the classroom at Sailing, Inc. The only part of the initial classroom instruction that I struggled with, quite literally, was knots. When we went out on the boats in the afternoon, I heeded the instruction of instructor Bill Corbett. "If you can't tie a knot," he said, "tie a lot."

I was sure I would feel comfortable once the boat was cruising along, and I was at the helm, steering, navigating, judging the wind. That was the part I always enjoyed: the proximity of nature, the feel of the boat under sail, the sights and sounds and smells of the sea.

Attaining this meditative state was not easy, however. First we had to prepare the boat's lines, check the equipment, and leave the harbor without incurring liability. Then we had to hoist the mainsail, trim the jib, adjust the boom, crank the winches and save the plastic buoy, which was constantly falling overboard.

Manning the helm was initially challenging as well. I was used to a tiller, which you turn the opposite direction of where you want the boat to head, while the boats at Sailing Inc. have wheels that operated similarly to car steering wheels – more or less.

At first most of us were oversteering. "It's not me," insisted Melisa, the first one at the helm. "The waves turn the boat." Peggy and I joked about not being able to control our cars after a week at the helm.

By midweek we were ready for an extended cruise. We sailed in two boats—myself, instructor Jerry Bancroft, Peggy and the Zornes aboard the forty-foot *Maklua* and the other five aboard the thirty-six-foot *Stray Days*. We headed toward the mouth of Resurrection Bay, rafted together, and anchored in Humpy Cove. Karen and Dave took the small kayaks off the bow of *Stray Days* and explored the cove more carefully; pink salmon were running and the host of fish swarming toward the nearby creek was an amazing sight.

Everyone eventually took a turn, and Peggy swore she would include kayaks on her boat.

"It's so peaceful," Mark Stearns said one evening. "The situation forces you to relax. There's nothing to do — no phone call to make, no meeting to attend. That's probably the most valuable part of the whole thing."

After barbecuing dinner, we'd sprawl around the decks and tell yarns — the sailing equivalent of sitting around the campfire. Bill Corbett recounted some of his private charters from hell.

First there were the two rotund brothers from New York who could capsize a boat just by seeking out each other's company. Then there were the buddies whose idea of provisions consisted of whisky and beer. Intoxicated, one of them picked a fight at a bonfire, almost killed himself boarding, then topped off the evening by hurling on the deck. Naturally, he didn't remember being sick the next morning and refused to clean up the mess.

We weren't quite as lucky with the weather the next day. While it was still sunny — "the weather was pretty awesome for Seward," Doug noted — the wind had died. It took most of the day to travel around Fox Island to the aptly named Sunny Cove, where we anchored for the night.

A couple of rough-looking participants in the Seward Salmon Derby were anchored nearby. After dinner, they puttered over in a skiff. "Excuse me," one inquired, "but would you have any Grey Poupon?"

As we sailed the first three days, some competition developed between the two boats. Especially when the women were at the helm. I was interested in cruising around and enjoying the scenery, and Doug Zornes seemed like-minded. But Milisa and Peggy wanted to race whenever we came close to our fellow students on *Stray Days*.

CHAPTER SIXTEEN

Bill Corbett enjoys racing too, and he encouraged the Stearns brothers and the Summerfeldts to steal our wind and cut us off whenever possible. According to witnesses, the precise nautical jargon he used was: "Chase them down and punish them like the dogs they are."

We spent the last few days aboard the boats cruising around the islands near the mouth of the bay and anchoring in quiet coves. A bonus of the class was that all the participants were enthusiastic and friendly. Peggy seemed the most motivated, probably because she was determined to buy a boat soon. A trained biologist, she thought over the "work to live, live to work" conundrum and concluded that she'd rather be a bartender. As such she was a professional at giving and taking grief as well as mixing kamikazes.

Doug and Milisa Zornes ran a computer company in Anchorage and enjoyed diving as well as sailing. They dove in temperate climes as well as chill Alaska waters. Still, they looked at me a bit strangely when I'd jump overboard and take a quick swim in the evening.

The Stearns brothers were seeming opposites—Mark an outgoing urban professional, Paul a quiet rural resident—but obviously close. And Dave and Karen Summerfeldt were in many ways the life of the party. Both enjoyed teasing Bill, their laid-back instructor who, Dave claimed, could hear a bag of peanut M&Ms rattling anywhere on the boat.

We studied for the last three exams while aboard. "It was a hard-working vacation," Doug said. And Dave added, "The more I learn and the more I read, the more I realize how much there is to know."

The material included engine repair and other technical aspects of sailing. Most of the others were handy and easily grasped the material. I'm decidedly unhandy and generally avoid any dealings with engines. I'm an English teacher, after all—I fix broken sentences, not carburetors, and I barely passed the tests.

There were laughs fueled by the "swillable red" wine aboard *Stray Days,* and silences fostered by the nearby mountains and sea. I think there is a harmony of the individual in nature and a harmony of the individual in a community, and when the two harmonies coincide, it makes for a beautiful experience.

We were tired but content when we returned to Seward. I think it was the fatigue that made me vulnerable when Peggy and I were hosing down *Maklua.* Doug and Milisa were below, and the crew of *Stray Days* came motoring along, seemingly lost, asking us where their slip was located.

They had us cold—fifteen feet away standing still. They threw their water balloons simultaneously but didn't even come close, though one of the balloons splashed the feet of a sailor on a boat behind us. What was there left to say? All we could offer was a scouting report of sorts: "Good sail, no arm."

17

They worked as a team to shove Cristina's truck into a tree.

From Seward I went to visit Fern and Ann Chandonnet in Anchorage. While there I received a call from the outgoing superintendent in the Gateway district, asking if I'd meet a teacher he just hired for the Tetlin elementary school position. I called the teacher and asked her to meet me at 6 p.m. under the grizzly bear head in the Regal Alaskan Hotel in Anchorage.

I should have seen trouble coming when she walked into the lobby—I couldn't believe the young woman striding toward me at the appointed hour had graduated from high school, much less college.

Her name was Cristina Welker. And like the heroine of the Jimmy Buffett song *Fins*, she's a Cincinnati girl who moved to a remote town and soon found herself surrounded by the sharks in the local bars, although these sharks were the Alaska rather than Florida variety.

Which is to say, hungrier.

She wasn't quite twenty-two, could pass for sixteen, and she was my new colleague—and technically, my employee. We sat outside on that cool July evening and became acquainted while we sipped amber beers and watched floatplanes take off and land on Lake Hood.

Cristina said she'd been curious about Alaska for many years and occasionally threatened to move north. Of course she stunned her family and friends when she actually made the move. "They're very supportive," she said, "but they think I'm nuts."

My mission that evening was to provide a balanced picture of life in a Native Alaska village. In my previous village job in Gambell, I'd seen several young teachers go from sunny idealists to bitter cynics in a matter of months. So I wanted to diminish her naivete without damaging her dream.

Later, a man with more experience in the area told me I should have scared the hell out of her and sent her packing for a kinder, gentler village. Bush communities in general are not compatible with first-year teachers of suburban sensibilities, and I learned after the fact that Tetlin is somewhat rougher than most.

It quickly became evident that to survive her Alaskan adventure, Cristina would have to fight on two fronts: in the classroom and anywhere a man decided to hit on her.

I should mention that while we became good friends, I never had any romantic interest in Cristina. And the feeling, or lack thereof, was mutual. Some reasons included the sixteen-year gap in our ages and my ethical belief that there should be a grace period before a supervisor hits on a staff member. In addition, while Cristina is very attractive, she's not my type. She's a pixyish blond with flawless features, and I tend to fall for tall brunettes with crooked noses.

Do I protest too much? Methinks not. Methought of her, in fact, as a kid sister: someone I cared about and felt protective towards. And given the confines of village life, it was lucky that we got along so well, both personally and professionally. We helped each other through some rough times.

Helping both of us was our colleague, the esteemed Dr. Stephen "Ole" Olson—a half-blind fiftyish lawyer, gold-miner, photographer and teacher. He'd spent six years teaching in Tetlin before we arrived, and he knew the kids and village very well. He also possessed a paradoxical attitude that was at once deeply caring and laid-back in the full-recline position. He'd seen scores of teachers come and go, and initially he was dubious about me and wasn't sure if Cristina would survive the first week, much less the year.

It certainly was a hell week for the new recruit. The children in her class punched her, cussed her, threatened her cat and generally created havoc. I tried to help, but had my own hands full with the high school kids. Cristina survived, albeit barely, and when she stumbled out of work on Friday and vowed to come back for more, Ole put the odds on her lasting the year at 50-50.

I thought she had a better chance because I'd glimpsed her underlying toughness. She was an athlete, after all, a rugby player who could hold her own in a scrum and displayed a bumper sticker on her door that read, "Support your local hooker—play rugby." She also wore a red jacket with "hooker" emblazoned on the sleeve, and I saw her—smiling and pleasant but not taking any guff —explain to an inquiring smartass that hooker was her rugby position, not her occupation. She offered to tackle him if he harbored any doubts.

By the third week of school, Cristina had control of her class. She still had tough days, to be sure, but I knew she'd be okay when I took one of my daily walks by her room and heard her yelling at the kids. Her voice resounded off the walls in that authoritarian pitch a teacher must acquire, and the sound put a smile on my face.

On weekends, needing a respite from village life, we'd head to Fairbanks or, more often, to Tok. The social scene in such places was interesting from the start. Five minutes after Cristina first walked into a watering hole in Tok, for example, the bar in front of her was lined with enough drinks to kill a hockey team.

I'd guess that close to thirty guys hit on Cristina in September alone. Old guys, young guys, fat guys, thin guys, white guys, black guys, Indian guys, Eskimo guys, single guys, married guys, divorced guys — the whole gamut of that rugged and endearingly hopeful Alaskan male took a shot at the new kid in town.

On the surface it's a situation some women might envy: a couple of dozen men vying for your affection can be flattering. But such persistent pursuit can be draining on a polite young woman. Who wants to spend the week managing kids and the weekends misdirecting men?

At first Cristina thought most of the men were just being friendly. We had some interesting debates about what constituted an actual hit. Was the guy who sent her a dozen gallons of drinking water hitting on her? The one who sketched her weekly nature pictures? How about the guy who let her shoot his gun? The one who gave her a boat ride? Or maybe the young man who drove fifty miles over the most treacherous road in North America just to watch Monday Night Football with her?

Then there was the pilot who changed her flat tire. Cristina claimed he was a friend and his motives were pure, but I knew better. Changing a tire is not a friend thing; a friend refers you to Mr. Goodwrench. And a guy who spins a woman's lug nuts is hoping for some reciprocity.

Yeah, every man within a hundred-mile radius had high hopes at first, including the village men. One came by her house on a Friday night when I happened to be watching her cat and some of her videos.

"Cristina here?" he inquired, looking around me.

"No, she went to Tok for the weekend.

"What are you doing here?" he asked suspiciously.

"Watching a movie and eating popcorn."

"Oh, I came to invite her duck hunting on the big lake tomorrow morning."

"That's nice of you," I said. "I'll tell her you came by. She won't be back until late Sunday night."

"Oh, Okay." He began walking away, then turned and made a friendly gesture. "You could maybe go duck hunting with us, John...if we have enough room on the boat." Naturally, there wasn't enough room on the boat. Not that I wanted to shoot a duck anyway. Nor did I think it would be wise to travel to a lake in the middle of nowhere with a heavily-armed man who assumed I was competition for Cristina.

The pursuit continued over the winter, and came to a head when Cristina slid off an icy road in her truck. She called the Tok Lodge from a nearby house and asked if anyone could give her some help. Rory, the owner-bartender, related the request, and the five regulars in the bar casually but immediately made excuses why they had to get home. All pretense ended when they neared the door—they broke into a sprint and began elbowing, pushing and clawing their way outside, each hoping to be the first hero on the scene. They ran to their trucks, peeled out of the parking lot, and had a drag race down Borealis Street. They arrived at roughly the same time and began trying out various theories of ditch extraction—which ended with them working as a team to shove Cristina's truck into a tree.

Now to put things in perspective, it must be stated that some of Cristina's allure is due to the Alaska Scale. This concept was introduced to me by my sportswriter friend Mike Taylor soon after I moved to the state. "You don't think you'll be affected by the scale," Mike said, "but you will be. Your standards get eroded here." He was telling a depressing truth: for the heterosexual Alaska male, it's always closing time.

I realize, by the way, that a scale which judges the bodily virtues of women is inherently sexist. But this is Alaska, where correct attitudes get frozen out in favor of reality, and I'd say the men here utilize the Scale almost as much as duct tape. Furthermore, I recall watching a movie with some women friends a few years back who blithely rated the actors' butts in a similar manner.

So let's crunch the numbers. If we were in the contiguous states, I would rank Cristina a solid "eight" (a "ten" being Cindy Crawford). This puts her right up there with Cindy on the Alaska Scale, which is at least two points more generous to women. The scale becomes increasingly generous the farther out in the Bush you go. Thus, in a village or remote town such as Tok, where fresh-faced single women are as rare as moon rocks, Cristina is off the scale. *Any* woman gets five additional points simply for showing up.

Given her rare status, Cristina had some unwanted passes from some undesirable guys. Since we hung out together fairly often, we developed a system of sorts. If she wanted to be alone with a guy, she wouldn't say anything and

I'd leave. If she wanted me to stick around, the code word was "Tiki," the name of her cat.

She mentioned the cat quite often that first year (but not around Dana, the aforementioned pilot).

Many of the hopefuls noticed that I tended to be in Cristina's orbit fairly often; a few took a dislike to me on this basis alone. I felt lucky to avoid a Cristina-inspired fistfight during the course of the year.

Some days I thought my life would have been easier – not to mention safer—if Cristina was two-eighty and had a face like a grizzly. Most days, though, I thought life in Tetlin was more bearable because this spirited young woman decided to have herself an adventure.

One evening as we were walking out of school and admiring the aurora borealis and a spray of stars, Cristina punched me on the arm. "I don't want to get all mushy or anything," she said, "but I really appreciate your friendship."

So okay, if she had a flat on that particular night, I might have lent a hand.

18

I usually don't allow students to call me a schmuck,
but with Allen, things were different.

In addition to Ole and Cristina, I quickly developed good
working relationships with Stan, the school's custodian, and
Rowena, the secretary and assistant teacher. My relationship
was not as good with the school's cook, who came late, left
early, and cooked badly.

Stan first brought Cristina and I into the village by skiff —
the road was a muddy morass in the summer. We enjoyed
scooting along the Tetlin River in the district's boat, winding
around the serpentine bends, viewing the hills and Mentasta
Mountains in the distance. We didn't even mind getting stuck
on a few sandbars; the boat came equipped with a long
wooden pole, and my first duty as principal-teacher was to
push us back into open water.

I soon learned that Stan was a computer enthusiast. Some
days he'd bring his iMac computer from his house to the school
in Tetlin, so he could use the Internet, and it was always entertaining to see him pushing a wheelbarrow containing this
modern piece of electronic gadgetry: a symbol of the old world
meeting the new.

CHAPTER EIGHTEEN

Rowena, I quickly learned, was intelligent, organized and had a great way with the kids. I thought she would have been an excellent teacher, and told her so many times. She'd had a little college, and we encouraged her to complete the degree and get her teaching license — but she seemed to lack the confidence for some reason. This was unfortunate, because the kids in Tetlin would have benefited from a Native teacher; and I think that's true of kids in every other Native village as well.

Alaska adopted a standards program while I was in Tetlin. The goal was to improve student learning, as measured on standardized tests, one of which would determine whether students would graduate from high school. Neither Ole nor I had much use for most of the standards — we didn't appreciate the infringement on our autonomy and creativity as teachers. We also knew that, barring a miracle, our students simply did not have a realistic chance of passing the graduation requirement. Too many had special education needs, too many were unmotivated, too many were far behind.

Our mutual goal was to simply improve our students' reading, writing, math and social skills. The "standard" we taught to was Marie Easton, a seventh grader and the brightest student in the school. We figured if Marie could not grasp the material, it was definitely too tough for the others.

Sometimes the lack of student achievement could make us cynical. At breakfast in the school kitchen, for example, Ole would often remark, "Remember John, where there's no hope, there's no hurry." His actions spoke louder – he worked long hours and was very animated and enthusiastic in the classroom.

It was touching to see the relationship Ole had with Allen "Skippy" Taylor, a developmentally disabled 18-year-old with a heart of gold. Every day after school Allen would walk into Ole's room and ask, "Game of chess, Ole?" Ole would make a show of thinking it over, then say, "Sure, Skippy." They'd been playing for years, and although Allen never beat Ole, he could give him a decent game. Allen's I.Q. was such that he should not have been capable of playing chess, much less playing well. But he had a window of intelligence that was enhanced through repetition, joy, and the patient guidance of a good teacher.

After the chess match, Allen would wander into my office. "How you doing, Schmuck?" he'd ask.

"Okay, Putz," I'd reply.

This was our traditional greeting; I'm not sure how it got started; perhaps Ole told him to "go into John's office and ask the schmuck how he's doing." I usually don't allow students to call me a schmuck or other derogatory names, but with Allen, things were different.

Following our greeting, I'd read him the latest NBA news on the Internet. Allen loved basketball almost as much as chess. And despite partial blindness and other physical limitations, he also loved to play the game. I had concerns about him being injured, and wanted to make him team manager. Allen was determined to play, however, and I relented when I saw the positive example he set. He'd get hit in the head with the basketball a dozen times each practice, but he never quit, never complained, never missed a day.

Although he only played a minute or so each game, if that, Allen was in many ways the heart of the team—and the village. The other students could be tough on any kid who was smaller and weaker, but with Allen there was a line they wouldn't cross. They might take his walking cane, but they would eventually give it back; they might lob a basketball at him, but they'd never hit him too hard. This peculiar attitude was illustrated one day in the gym, when Allen accidentally ran into a girl and knocked her down. He simply didn't see her, but she jumped up and punched him in the nose, then ran for her life as a dozen outraged kids gave chase.

Because of Allen's poor eyesight, Ole walked him home every night—a tad ironic because Ole couldn't see so well himself. To me, there was something ineffably moving about watching the lanky Norwegian and the squat Athabascan, with perhaps one good eye between them, walking slowly homeward. Jean Vanier wrote that people with handicaps are capable of awakening what is most precious in a human being, and I think Allen Taylor awakened something in Ole— and in everyone else who knew him.

19

It's a sin to kill a mockingbird, but you can shoot
a ptarmigan in the head.

The Tetlin Indian Reservation is sublime. On fall week-ends I enjoyed taking long, leisurely hikes through the nearby hills. Sometimes, if a grizzly was spotted in the area, I'd bor-row Ole's shotgun. And on one such day I used said gun to shoot a ptarmigan.

The Willow Ptarmigan is Alaska's state bird, probably as the result of a collective brain fart on the part of the Ter-ritorial Legislature in the 1950s. Overall, the Legislature did well by Alaska, endowing the state with a lovely flower (For-get-Me-Not), noble tree (Sitka Spruce), inspiring motto ("North to the Future") and a beautiful flag (Big Dipper and North Star on a dark blue background).

I'm not sure why the Legislature settled for the ptarmi-gan – also known as *Lagopus lagopus* or Tundra Turkey. The bird is ugly, annoying and can barely fly.

But it does taste pretty good over noodles.

Yes, Alaskans eat the state bird. Am I the only one who thinks this strange? I believe the willow ptarmigan is the lone state bird to be "honored" in this fashion. You certainly don't hear about Wisconsinites eating robins, New Yorkers eating bluebirds or Marylanders eating Baltimore Orioles – not even if they drop a double-header.

"It's part of the Alaska charisma," suggested Leigh Tutterrow, a wildlife technician with the Alaska Department of Fish and Game. "Sort of a mountain man thing." She added that from August through March, a hunter can take ten ptarmigan a day and have up to twenty in his or her possession. So while other state birds are pursued by ornithologists carrying cameras, the willow ptarmigan is pursued by hunters carrying guns. Doesn't this suggest a certain lack of respect for a state symbol? I mean, taking potshots at those dangerous road signs is one thing, but the Alaska bird? Of course the ptarmigan isn't exactly respected prey; the birds all but wears signs saying, "Shoot me."

"You can walk right up on that bird," a friend told me. "They just sit there and wait for you to make 'em supper." To make the hunt more interesting, my friend and many other Alaskans carry handguns when pursuing ptarmigan—and aim for the head. Body shots are just too easy. This has led to an Alaskan twist on an old saying. "It's a sin to kill a mockingbird," the saying goes, "but you can shoot a ptarmigan in the head."

To be fair, I must note that ptarmigans do have enough sense to disguise themselves. They turn brown in the summer, white in winter, and a brown-white combination during transition periods. This, by the way, is why Alaska hunters shoot the occasional cocker spaniel during the autumn months. Fluffy wanders onto the tundra and, BANG, another ptarmigan-inspired tragedy.

But I digress. The topic was disguise. According to the *Field Guide to the Birds of North America*, the ptarmigan's camouflage is undermined by its "croaks" and "noisy cackles." And during mating season, the guide said, male ptarmigans make a "raucous" noise that sounds like "go back, go back, go back." Obviously the female ptarmigans don't take this to heart, or *Lagopus lagopus* would be long lost, both as a species and as a reluctant single guy. This could also be the reason why male willow ptarmigans are known for staying close by their families. The males tell the females to "go back" when it's time to mate, and thereafter the females tell the males to "stick around if you know what's good for you, *Lagopus*."

While I'm not much of a hunter, I did like the idea of consuming a state symbol. So I walked the hills and kept a keen eye for any *Lagopus lagopus* lurking about.

I was sweating when I reached the top of the long hill. I stopped to rest and looked back at the village — the school, the houses in neat rows, the twisting river. I set off through the burn left by the Tok River Fire in 1990. I was about four miles from the village when I saw a ptarmigan perched on a branch in one of the skeletal trees.

I raised the shotgun as the ptarmigan took wing. He was, naturally, flying slowly and directly toward me — as if auditioning for the Endangered Species List. He landed in a tree about ten feet away. "Go back," he said, and I retreated a couple of steps for the sake of sport. "Go back," he repeated. "No way," I replied, and pulled the trigger. He fell to the ground and I placed him in my pack.

That evening I mixed the breast meat with cream of mushroom soup and ate the state bird over egg noodles, savoring every bite. While cleaning up afterward, I thought some more about the bird and its unfortunate name. *Ptarmi-*

gan. Easy to shoot, tough to say. Right now some readers, not aware that the "p" is silent, are saying the word as "pit-arm-again." The subconscious recognizes this as nonsense, though, and logically rearranges the word as "armpit-again." This is why many people associate Alaska's state bird with a damp, smelly, shadowy thing that requires daily attention.

Lagopus lagopus—the bird isn't even capable of flying south for the winter. Louisiana has the brown pelican. New Mexico has the roadrunner. Do we really want the Last Frontier represented by a dim, loud, hard-to-say cooking bird akin to the chicken?

The only state bird that approaches the lowly standard set by the willow ptarmigan is the Hawaiian goose, which made me wonder if they ran out of decent birds by the time the last states joined the union. Research indicated this was not the case. At the very least Alaska could have shared a bird, as there is ample precedent. Consider that seven states claim the cardinal, six claim the meadowlark, five the mockingbird and three the robin. And Maine and Massachusetts share the chickadee.

Alaska probably could have shared the eagle with the federal government (although some might say the forty-ninth state already shares too much with the Feds). We certainly have the better claim. I mean, when was the last time you heard of an eagle soaring over the nation's capital?

Some folks might nominate the mosquito as the Alaska state bird, given that we regularly bleed for this winged pest. My choice, though, would be the raven. This handsome and clever bird inspires legends. It is celebrated in verse by Edgar Allan Poe and was a scout for Noah. The Tlingit believe the raven is divine, and it has a place of honor atop their totem poles.

Furthermore, it's against the law to shoot a raven, in the head or elsewhere. We can all pronounce the name. And a raven can kick the willow out of ptarmigan.

A new century is upon us, and a change is in order. The willow ptarmigan has had a forty-three-year run – surely that's enough. The raven should be the state bird for the 21st Century.

And evermore.

20

Tundra Jesus would not catch-and-release.

I shared a house with Ole in Tetlin, while Cristina had one to herself next door. Early on, Ole explained that his marriage dynamic worked best if he spent the week in Tetlin and visited his family in Tok on the weekends.

The teacher houses, like those in Gambell, did not come equipped with bathrooms. The school bathroom was close enough that I didn't bother with a honey bucket; if I needed to relieve myself during the night, I merely peed off the porch. Ole, being somewhat more civilized, would walk down the steps and over to the woods, while Cristina, being a woman and far more civilized, would head to the school.

On clear nights I'd often see the waving aurora while emptying the bladder, and this always brought an awestruck-smile. During my years in Tetlin I was too often preoccupied with the future—where I'd be heading for the weekend or for my next job. But peeing off the porch, listening to the stream crackle in the frigid air while watching the heavenly lights, I was entirely in the moment, and I vowed to begin living the rest of my life in the present as well.

I'd have to laugh when my friends would send e-mails complaining about the fifteen-degree cold snap they were experiencing in Minneapolis or Chicago. Exaggerating slightly, I'd write back that you didn't know what cold was until it was fifty-below and you peed an icicle.

The extreme cold we sometimes endured in Tetlin was hard on man and beast alike. One morning at school I heard a terrible howling on the front deck, and went outside to find a dog with his tongue stuck to the steel grating. I went back into to get some hot water, which I thought might free him, but he was gone when I returned. His tongue, however, was still on the deck. We heard the dog was put down about an hour later; the tongue lasted two days.

The cold also had its good points. I skied nearly every day for five months, frequently with Ole and occasionally with Cristina. Ole didn't ski as often as I did, but he skied better, taking long, classical strides while I shuffled along in something resembling a jog. We carved out the trail in early November; it ran roughly north for three miles along the Tetlin River. Some of my best memories of Tetlin were the times when I'd simply ski away from my problems, gliding through long shadows cast by trees in the flat winter light, feeling ever more free as I moved deeper into the silent and rich splendor of the boreal forest.

I saw many animal tracks while skiing, including fox, hare, moose, caribou, lynx and bear. And a few times I saw tracks that I could not explain logically; they were bigger than any bear could have produced, and while my six-foot-five Norwegian colleague had big feet, he did not have BIG FEET.

Many people in Tetlin believed implicitly that Bigfoots (or is it Bigfeet?) roamed the area. One of my students claimed to have been abducted by a Bigfoot when she was a young girl and dropped on the outskirts of the village. Her claim was supported by her sister, and if such abductions were not commonplace in the village, they had, the locals said, occurred from time to time over the years. This was one reason villagers kept their windows shut during the summer months.

I had more concerns about Big Danny than Bigfoot. Big Danny Adams was Tetlin's chief, and at 6-foot-3 and 300-plus pounds, he lived up to his name. Our relationship was rocky from the start. He thought I treated his kids unfairly; I thought he demanded special treatment for his kids that wasn't fair to the others.

Our primary conflict concerned his oldest son, Willie. Willie was a fine basketball player, and I badly wanted him to play for the school team. The problem was that Willie didn't actually attend school more than a few days a year. To Big Danny, this wasn't an issue—he didn't see why education should stand in the way of basketball.

Sometimes Big Danny could be very charming and pleasant; other times he resorted to intimidation. I experienced the latter when I kicked his daughter April out of the gym because she hadn't been in school that day, which was the standard district policy. He came storming up to the school in a livid rage and directed some interesting adjectives at me. Then he threatened to have a guy in Fairbanks knock me off.

Not sure where the hit was to take place, I figured it was safest to stay in the village for a while and keep an eye out for passing Fairbanksans. Fortunately, Danny apologized a couple of weeks later, and apparently called off the hit—if there was one—which I appreciated.

Jim Elliott, the superintendent of the Gateway district, gave me helpful advice about placating Big Danny and other matters, though we didn't see eye to eye on everything. For example, when the toilet in the boys' bathroom became clogged when he was at the school, Jim was surprised that I grabbed a plunger. He noted that such duties should be performed by Stan Taylor, our custodian.

Stan was also postmaster of the village and spent much of the day at the post office. The post office did not have a phone, so Jim gave me some cheap walkie-talkies and told me to contact Stan if he was needed for cleanup or other duties. I had trouble keeping a straight face; I wasn't going to call Stan over to the school to plunge a clogged toilet or mop a little blood or do one of the other thirty-second custodial jobs we required during a typical day.

We did have fun with the walkie-talkies, though. When a plane from Forty-Mile Air was taxiing down the runway to the village, we'd report, "The Eagle has landed." And when Jim or another district honcho was on his way to Tetlin, I'd say, "Foley to Taylor, Liberty is moving, I repeat, Liberty is moving."

I needed to find reasons to laugh in Tetlin. Village life was challenging, and I was going through a difficult time personally – in recent years I'd endured a failed marriage, my mother's passing, financial hardship, professional setbacks, and several pointless and unsettling moves.

I was looking for a fresh start spiritually. Assuming that I might survive Tetlin and live my allotted three-score and ten, I wanted the second half of my life to be more virtuous and purposeful than the first half. I'd drifted from the Catholicism of my youth – too many rules and regulations and guilt – and I had no interest in the intolerant (and sometimes in-your-face) fundamentalism predominant in Tok and many other communities in Alaska. I did admire Jesus, although I concluded that he was a tough act to follow. I also concluded that he would fit right in up north – Tundra Jesus, if you will.

With his long hair and beard, he'd look just like another one of those wilderness hippies you see in Talkeetna and Homer. Tundra Jesus wouldn't hunt, I don't think, but he'd be a helluva fisherman. Other anglers would marvel at his artistry and note that he'd sit quietly in the boat when he'd caught his limit; TJ would not catch-and-release.

I think Tundra Jesus would have a small cabin a few miles from town, with no lock on the door. His days would be spent hauling water and chopping wood, reading and tending his garden, meditating in silence and singing in praise. He'd have a pack of loyal strays following at his heels.

TJ would walk or ski to town, depending on the season, and smile and wave at the locals as he went about his business. He'd look you in the eye and tell you his truth, and even if you disagreed with him you'd admire his conviction of belief and clarity of thought. He'd never complain about the weather, and you'd feel better when he was around.

TJ would not be a regular at the local tavern, but he'd show up now and then, sip a little red wine, enjoy the music, nod in a friendly manner. He wouldn't have a girlfriend but the women would all love him.

I think Tundra Jesus would have been pissed off at Joe Hazelwood and the boys from Exxon—and he would have forgiven them.

Naturally TJ would be a good neighbor, quietly helping those in need: a pile of wood would appear on the porch of the old Sourdough, a pile of snow disappear from the driveway of the arthritic widow. And TJ would make a couple of bucks subbing at the nearby elementary school; he'd tell good stories and the kids would laugh with joy and chase after him as he left for the day...

Anyway, in addition to Christianity, I began to study other religions and philosophies, including Stoicism, Buddhism, and Mysticism. I'm sure this spiritual stew—a half-cup of this, a dash of that—offends some faithful followers. But I found nourishment and, in time, the path I had lost somewhere along the line.

21

"It's an Alaska tradition that the hunter bites the
head off the kill."

Ole hailed from a prominent Minnesota family, and he
was planning to become a lawyer in their construction business. He told me he was unhappy at the prospect, however, and decided to go his own way. He drifted around
the Northwest for a while before taking up gold mining
in the Forty-Mile; initially he exchanged labor for knowledge,
then began working his own claim. He was cagey about how
much gold he'd actually discovered over the years, although
he made it clear that he had yet to hit the proverbial Mother
Lode.

Fond of aphorisms, he said the key to gold mining—
and most of life's endeavors—was to "start from scratch
and keep on scratching." The mine was his sole occupation sometimes, and he and his wife Helen went through
some lean years before he started teaching in his forties;
sometimes they survived off what they found in the
dumpster behind the Tok grocery store.

To keep himself lean, Ole tried to adhere to his "bread
and water of affliction" diet while in Tetlin. Sometimes,
though, he'd spot something tempting in the kitchen trash

and salvage it for consumption. The first time he did this, Cristina and I were eating dinner, and she dropped her fork. "That is *so* gross!" she declared. Ole just smiled and heated up what he'd found in the microwave.

He seemed to get a kick out of shocking Cristina every now and then. Once when we went hiking in the Tetlin hills, Ole brought his shotgun along, and he let Cristina fire it when we spotted a ptarmigan in a tree. She nailed the bird, which fell from a tree branch, but was squeamish about picking it up. "No way am I touching that," she said. So Ole walked over, casually grabbed the dead bird by the neck, then offered it to Cristina, saying, "It's an Alaska tradition that the hunter bites the head off the kill." She recoiled in horror, much to his delight.

Still, Cristina and I enjoyed Ole's offbeat humor — after we got to know him. At first I didn't quite know how to take it when he said, with a straight face, "You know, John, two of the last three principal-teachers didn't leave the village alive." Our students were also subject to his strange wit. Once, for example, he blocked the entrance to the school following a fire drill. One of Cristina's students, Gage Easton, looked up at Ole in surprise. "This is a controlled entrance, buddy," Ole said to the mystified third grader. "You'll have to sing *Dixie* to gain entry. Come on, I'll help you. *I wish I was in the land of cotton...*"

Although Ole was one of the Tok fundamentalists, and we disagreed about most religious matters, we nevertheless managed to become friends. It helped that we shared similar views on teaching and were both bibliophiles...Actually, we could be literary snobs, and had trouble concealing a mild disdain for teachers who did not value books as much as we did.

In his years at the mine Ole had no television or other modern distractions, and he'd spent many hours reading many books. His taste ran to religion and political history – he liked to note the Viking conquest of Ireland circa 800 A.D. – and mine to fiction and journalism, but we both enjoyed poetry and philosophy.

Ole and Helen were also generous spirits who took in this wanderer for many meals when I was in Tok. Often I'd eat dinner with them and then drive out to Tetlin Sunday night with Ole. His old Ford pickup couldn't handle the rocky road very fast; our usual speed was under 20 mph. Some villagers took the road at 45 mph or faster, but that was dangerous, and on several occasions we were passed by vehicles that we later saw wedged against trees or half-flipped against snowbanks.

My least favorite part of our drives back to Tetlin was chaining up the tires before the Tetlin Hills. Ole kept heavy-duty chains in the bed of his truck, and I hated them with a passion. Attaching the chains meant, first, removing myself from the warm cab in sub-zero temperatures to crawl around under the truck and, second, taking off my gloves to get the doo-hickey linked to the thing-a-ma-jig. It only took me four months to master this skill.

All in all, I think Ole was probably the most complex man I've ever known. He was a rustic *and* a well-read intellectual; he did an hour of yoga in the morning *and* smoked cigarettes; he was a gold miner *and* prized nature; he was a conservative Christian *and* – in his younger years – consumed enough marijuana to be an honorary Jamaican.

As the lone liberal Democrat within 500 square miles (the predominant political affiliations being Republican and Redneck), I was sometimes annoyed by Ole's right-wing opinions and conspiracy theories, as well as the aforementioned religious intolerance. Mostly, though, I was impressed by the breadth of his mind. And after a time I realized that he was more tolerant than I'd initially thought.

Ole's teaching style was influenced by his legal training, and his primary tool was the lecture. This flew in the face of the research showing that lecturing was the worst way to teach young students, particularly lower-end and special-ed kids. That Ole's lecturing worked at all in Tetlin was a tribute to his entertaining style, a quick mind that could provide cogent examples, and his passion.

In truth, Ole was still far more passionate about gold; he hated being at school in the fall when he could still be working his mine. I had scant interest in gold mining before I met him, and after hearing about the arduous work involved, I had even less.

Usually Ole tried to recruit a partner to help him during the summer months at the mine. I think he quickly concluded that I would have made a terrible partner, because he never asked me. His partners over the years included his eldest son Gustav; a fundamentalist Christian who was built like an NFL lineman; and a violent ex-con who is no longer among the living.

The ex-con was a good partner, very loyal and hardworking. And while he could be violent with other men—Ole had seen him pull a knife a few times—he only threatened Ole once. The occasion was a prospecting mission gone bad. A fog settled over the Forty Mile River area, and when they tried to walk out, they became disoriented; they didn't have a compass and headed toward Canada rather than Tok. By the time Ole realized the error, they'd been walking several days and were out of food.

CHAPTER TWENTY-ONE

Finally, when they were growing weak, Ole proposed eating his partner's dog. He turned on Ole and said, "If you kill that dog, I'm gonna kill you!" The subject was dropped and, fortunately, they soon came upon a wilderness cabin that, in accord with Alaska tradition, was open and stocked.

His ex-con partner was killed a while later in a domestic incident at a remote cabin. Ole went with the Troopers to identify the body and bring it back to Tok.

After one year in Tetlin, I was ready to leave. I'd had conflicts with Big Danny and several other village parents over school policy, and I didn't need the aggravation. Several parents were also upset with me for supposedly manhandling their kids. Fights were an almost daily occurrence at the school, particularly among the younger kids, and they ignored verbal warnings to abate. The options left for me were to stand idly by while the kids beat each other bloody, thus incurring the wrath of their parents; or to step in and physically separate them, thus incurring the wrath of their parents. I couldn't win in Tetlin, and I found the situation frustrating.

Also, I was lonely. I'd dated a few women in Tok and Fairbanks, but did not see any long-term potential. So I told my colleagues that I was planning to head on down the highway.

Determined as I was to enter a post-guilt stage of my existence, I still succumbed on occasion. In this instance, Helen Olson made me feel mildly guilty by telling me she didn't want Ole to have to break in another principal; and Cristina made me feel deeply guilty by telling me she wouldn't return to Tetlin if I didn't.

Cristina had come a long way in nine months. She had all her students reading and doing their work, and the kids who initially terrorized her soon fell in love with her; when she walked around the village they came running from all directions to hug her and hang on her and hold her hand. It would have been a shame if the Pied Piper from Cincinnati hadn't returned to build on her work.

So I caved to guilt—and perhaps a little to hope—and came back for a second year.

22

To everyone's relief, the cutthroat competition for Cristina ended her second year.

The summer between my first and second years in Tetlin, I decided to have one last hitchhiking adventure. The decision was partly influenced by my beater car, which would not have survived the Alcan. In fact, I left the car at the school district offices in Tok and bummed rides from Ole in and out of the village, because I didn't think it would survive Tetlin Road.

Alaska is a great place to hitch rides, second only to Ireland in my experience. The Irish seem to feel guilty about passing up hitchhikers, and I think it helped that I have, as one woman put it, "the map of Ireland practically written on your face." Alaska, on the other hand, is a backpacker's Mecca in the summer months, and folks are very willing to give young—and in my case, not so young—adventurers a lift down the highway.

I had lots of thumbed miles under my belt by this time. I'd started hitching rides when I was a teen and needed to travel to neighboring towns to find decent basketball competition. I'd continued to hitchhike into my twenties and thirties, and traveled through most of Western Europe and the Western U.S. via thumb.

I met many wonderful people and never had any serious problems hitchhiking — although a Frenchman scared the hell out of me. He and his wife decided to have some drinks on the way north from Spain, you see, and they were pleased to have me join the party. He had a mini-bar in his trunk and he'd stop every twenty miles or so and freshen the drinks.

As might be expected, his driving became progressively worse. I vividly recall sitting in the backseat holding a gin and tonic as he made a blind pass around a truck — and almost hit another head-on. He saw my terror-stricken face in his rearview mirror and uttered one of his few English phrases: "Take it easy, Baby!"

Anyway, I decided to call it quits as a hitchhiker after the summer. I was simply getting too old — there is something more than a little pathetic about a guy with a graying beard and expanding middle standing on the side of the road with his thumb out, trying to look unthreatening.

Still, my thumb served me well on its farewell tour. I bummed around Washington, California, Utah and Montana for a couple of months, then visited family in Minnesota. When I returned to Tok in mid-August, several people around town were surprised to see me. I later heard that a few folks made a bet that I would find an excuse to stay Outside, despite my promise to Ole and Cristina and my contract with the school district.

I knew the kids and village better my second year, and generally things went smoother. I was more flexible and felt comfortable deviating from the schedule occasionally. For instance, I liked to paint watercolors in my free time, and I would usually hold an impromptu art class once a week. Many of the young people in Tetlin had artistic ability, and they appreciated this quiet time to express themselves.

Living in a village, it was important to get along with the kids who were not model students — and I suppose that's a fine idea even if you don't live in a village. I tried to convey that while I might get on them about their classroom behavior and school work, I held no hard feelings.

A case in point were two young men in the high school. I had to reprimand Royalyn Mark and Little Billy Sam on an almost daily basis. But at lunch, I tried to make a point of shooting hoops with them; basketball was their great love, and was once mine, and without saying anything it was understood that playing HORSE was a kind of mutual forgiveness for our classroom conflicts.

They could flat-out shoot, too. It wasn't uncommon for Billy to hit ten or fifteen jumpers in a row from outside the three-point line, and we usually split our games. Royalyn only beat me once, and he did it with an amazing shot that he'd been practicing for years. We were tied at "S" apiece when he took the ball and, standing under the basket, hurled it with an underhand motion toward the gym wall just beyond the sideline. On the ricochet the ball rose in an arc from the corner and swished cleanly through the net. Royalyn said, "Yes!" and ran around the gym with his arms raised in triumph. He knew I couldn't duplicate that shot.

Another challenging student was Annie Lyons, who was pregnant my first year in Tetlin and brought her infant son to class the second year. I admired her determination to finish high school, as well as her maturity and the value she placed on her Athabascan ancestry. She wrote some wonderful essays about learning the old language and traditions from her grandmother, and it was clear to me that Annie would be the torchbearer for her generation—and probably a village leader.

Still, Annie didn't always feel that the school rules should apply to her, and she had a temper. We had our share of conflicts. And yet I think she understood that Ole, Cristina and I were trying to help her on her journey. It always comforted me to think of conflicts with my students as mere farts—bad air that passes.

To everyone's relief, the cutthroat competition for Cristina ended her second year. She made it very clear that she was with Dana, the aforementioned pilot. And in September she discovered she was pregnant as well. They were very happy and made plans to marry.

I was a little nervous myself, especially as Cristina began to waddle in March and April. A small village such as Tetlin lacks the medical personnel and facilities for childbirth, naturally, and I had a recurring nightmare in which Cristina, in obvious pain, waddled into my office at school and announced: "The baby is coming." This was followed by me taking charge: "Ole, boil water! Stan, tear up white sheets! Rowena, call Forty-Mile Air and have them send a plane, I'm getting the hell outta here!"

Thankfully, Cristina arranged to take some time off from work well before her due date, and gave birth to a lovely baby girl named Caily in a Fairbanks hospital.

23

Sometimes the Irish charm works, sometimes it doesn't.

On my own monthly trips to Fairbanks, I'd typically catch a movie and visit friends. One Halloween I decided to check out the festivities at The Howling Dog saloon outside of town. I was dancing with a young woman—or at least shuffling my feet to the musical beat—when I was shoved hard in the back; I lost my balance and almost fell.

I was angry when I turned to confront the man who pushed me. He was unapologetic, and I said a few cross words. He retorted in kind. And then we began striking each other in the face with our fists, as men are wont to do when they collide on dance floors. The ritual goes way back; I don't think it has a name, but "break-face dancing" aptly describes it.

We were separated and the singer told us to take it outside. Suddenly I felt childish and, expecting the worst, tentatively extended my hand to my adversary. He shook it and the singer commended us. Still, I thought it best to take my leave. I was aware, of course, that educators are held to a higher standard of public behavior, and I was envisioning newspaper headlines: "Principal Pummeled in Barroom Brawl" had a nice ring. "Tetlin Teacher in Tussle" worked well, too. An accompanying editorial might read, "Higher Education in the Howling Dog."

The fight would have been avoided altogether if we were dressed for the occasion, like most of the other patrons in the bar. You just don't scuffle with Count Dracula. And only the lowest of men will take a swing at a guy in a gorilla costume.

Most of my visits to Fairbanks were more serene. Usually I'd visit my Bounding friends Rod Boyce and Julie Stricker, who found jobs as editors with the *Fairbanks Daily News-Miner* after *The Anchorage Times* turned turtle. They bought a beautiful log home on a nice parcel of land off Chena Hot Springs Road, made friends, planted a garden, filled a kennel with energetic dogs, took up mushing, and generally seemed to live in idyllic splendor.

Mushing, however, is not for the faint of heart, and they've both suffered mishaps. Julie once crashed a sled into a tree and was banged up pretty badly, including bruises on her face. "People were giving Rod dirty looks for a while," she joked.

Not to be outdone, Rod scared the hell out of all of us when he disappeared during a two-hundred mile race on the Kenai Peninsula. As it turned out, Rod missed a turn after leaving the checkpoint at Caribou Lake, about fifty miles into the Tustumena 200.

It was shortly after midnight when he left Caribou Lake, and he ran his ten-dog team about forty-five minutes after the missed turn. Rod then spent several hours trying to reaquire the trail. Finally he acknowledged that he was lost and made camp along a ridge with his ten dogs.

Meanwhile, a storm had moved in and was growing progressively worse; snow and winds up to 50 mph left eight-foot drifts among the hills, closed Sterling Highway on the west side of the Kenai, and triggered avalanches. Rod stayed put for two days as the storm continued to rage. He cared for the dogs, built fires, rationed food, and pondered a plan of action when he wasn't thinking about Julie.

By the third day, Rod's food consisted of one bag of Reese's Bites. The dogs were stressed by lack of food and the foreign landscape, and Rod spent much of his time trying to keep them settled. He stayed on the ridge because he knew a search was underway, and that it is best to stay put when lost in the wilderness.

He had some fearful thoughts; early on he cried one night and begged aloud to be rescued or provided a way out. "I'll be a better husband. Please get me out of here." He calmed himself and thought with bitter humor about a news editor becoming a news story.

On the fourth day he organized the camp and took off again. He made another ridge by 11:30 a.m., and looked at the Kenai Mountains to the east. A short time later his eyes fixed on a mark that seemed out of place, about four miles away. He saw it was a snowmachiner. Another soon followed, and Rod, filled with new hope, began walking toward the distant trail.

He made it to the trail, and about forty-five minutes later was found by snowmachiner Ron Poston. Volunteers quickly organized and saved the dogs, which, apart from being tired and hungry, were all fine. Rod was initially taken to Caribou Lake Lodge, and then flown by Troopers to Soldotna, where he was reunited with Julie.

The story made worldwide news, and Rod was besieged by the media. He wrote a fine story about the experience and let it drop, turning down requests for interviews and television reenactments.

I had no interest in mushing myself, but I got to know a half-dozen sled dogs fairly well when I took care of a kennel for a woman friend in Fairbanks. I was actually set up with her by Rod and Julie. She was very intelligent and pleasant, but unfortunately had no interest in a romantic relationship once she got to know me—sometimes the Irish charm works, sometimes it doesn't. We became friends, though, and she asked me to look after her kennel while she was away for two weeks in the summer.

I took exquisite care of her dogs. I fed them, watered them and cleaned up the kennel on a regular basis. While working such chores one morning, I also stepped in a hole and sacrificed myself on an altar of husky hair, dog chow, mud and crap. The dogs seemed to appreciate this show and howled with something that sounded like glee.

One evening I returned from town to find sled dog Chopper having his way with sled dog Jute. All the dogs had loose collars and could escape their chains with a little effort; in the throes of passion, Chopper had done so. I made the sorry assumption that my friend would have warned me to alert her if this was a problem, so I merely returned young stud Chopper to his collar and chain and more or less forgot about the incident.

Puppies were not part of my friend's future plans, and she went ballistic when she heard the news. And I decided minimize my future dealings with sled dogs.

24

If you have any kind of problem, an Alaskan will be the first to help. And if you cause problems, an Alaskan will be the first to shoot you.

Before leaving Fairbanks to return to Tetlin, I'd usually stock up on food for the school. This was especially imperative when we hosted the annual Tetlin Basketball Tournament. I took the school district's eighteen-passenger van on those occasions and packed every inch of it with food and drinks.

The van—which I affectionately called the Great White Elephant Van—served us well on school trips, although we had more than a few problems. On one winter trip, for example, the side door slid off its track in Nenana. It was a Sunday and no repair shops were open. I tried to wire it shut, without luck; it fell off again. We drove to Fairbanks with our heater fighting a losing battle against the minus thirty-degree temperatures that slipped through the gaps in the sliding door. Students took turns holding the door in place; we gave them extra gear for the five-minute door duty. "Okay, time to rotate," I'd announce when I saw the student holding the door start to shiver. "Give Theresa the big mitten."

In Fairbanks, a student accidentally let go of the door and it fell off near Bentley Mall. I had words with the door as I tried to jam it back in place. A man carving an ice angel on a nearby corner came over and, using his carving tools, managed to get the door back on track. I thanked him profusely. He exemplified the positive side of the Alaskan dichotomy: if you have any kind of problem, an Alaskan will be the first to help you. And if you cause any kind of problem, an Alaskan will be the first to shoot you.

On a spring trip in the van, I pulled into an Anchorage parking garage and started up the ramp. I was looking in the rear-view mirror at some kids wrestling in the back seats, telling them to knock it off, when I heard a terrible noise. It was fingernails on a chalkboard, a wail of agonizing pain, a cacophony of rap and heavy metal bands. It was, in fact, the luggage rack on top of the van being half-wrenched off by a collision with a concrete beam. I stomped the brake; the kids, in the wake of the evil noise, were quiet for a few deadly seconds. Then someone laughed. I told him it wasn't funny. This triggered more laughter, another threat from me, and then I surrendered and laughed as well. Sometimes things are so bad you can't do anything else.

The most memorable trip in the Great White Elephant Van involved several basketball games at schools several hundred miles apart. Why go so far to play basketball? Two reasons: not enough small school teams locally, and the opportunity for our rural students to see the "big city," otherwise known as Anchorage.

The trip began on a Thursday afternoon in Tetlin. We arranged rides for the players from the village to Tok via Tetlin Road, a marathon of hellish holes, treacherous turns, and improbable inclines. Having survived the first part of the journey, we confidently loaded the team into the van.

Unfortunately, all our gear would not fit inside. So we tossed the bags into the rack on top, picked up four large pizzas at Fast Eddy's, and set off down the Glenn Highway.

We were three miles out of Tok when I saw something hit the road behind us; it seemed unlikely the object dropped from the heavens, so I turned the van around in a mere eight moves on the two-lane highway. Sure enough, most of our gear was littering the road back to town, creating an obstacle course for the few drivers out that evening. One kindly man even picked up a few of our bags before they became roadkill.

"Bernoulli's Effect," said Ole, who was riding shotgun. I thought he was commenting on the pizzas, but he explained that it was a scientific principle involving air currents which create pressure on objects such as gym bags and principals.

While we were atop the van securing our gear in sub-zero temperatures, the students inside grew impatient. So they began rocking the van. Upon reflection I realized that, when I was their age, I would have rocked away with vigor and glee. At the moment, though, I was gripping the rack and flopping around like a fish on a line, while threatening them with suspension and sandwiches. "No McDonald's for you, you little shitheads!"

Now I should note that I would never encourage educators to use obscenities in front of students, much less direct such language *at* them. But it's always worked for me.

We were on the road again shortly. When we reached the Alaska Range, we encountered a blizzard. I slowed to under 40 mph and we continued toward Glennallen. Ole helped by providing commentary while I drove. He told me about a man I'd seen limping around Tok. The man limped as a result of a gunshot wound sustained years before, Ole explained. He'd been present in the rural tavern when the guy shot another man in the hand. The wounded man said, "You shot me, now I'm gonna shoot you," and fired into his adversary's foot. Hence the limp...and the term "Frontier Justice."

Ole's poor eyesight prohibits him from driving outside a fifty-mile radius of Tok; I suppose they think he knows the roads around Tok well enough by feel. In any case, I was stuck with the driving burden. We reached Glennallen safely and bunked our co-ed, pre-to-post adolescent team in three rooms at the Caribou Hotel annex. I stayed with the high school boys, Ole stayed with the junior high boys, and we gave the five girls on the team a room to themselves.

Both Ole and I believe in giving kids some freedom. At least that's how we rationalized our reluctance to stop the card playing and attendant gambling in which they engaged until the wee hours. We knew that any money wagered would at least stay within the village. We also knew that kids need to let off some steam or the pressure cooker explodes, and this is especially ugly if the pressure cooker is a Great White Elephant Van rolling down an icy road.

We rounded up the kids around 2 a.m. and they were asleep in minutes. Early the next morning, Curtis Sam, a four-foot-four sixth-grader, opened our door. He looked at the three snoring high school bodies sprawled about the room. Then he inquired, in a voice that compensates in volume for what it lacks in depth, "You guys still sleeping?"

"Run, Curtis," I advised as the older boys began to stir and mumble threateningly. "It's good for your health."

We had a late afternoon game against Cornerstone Christian in Palmer, so we continued down the highway. The mountainous stretch of road north of Sutton caused some anxiety among the students.

"We slid into the ditch right there a few years ago," Angela said.

"I hit my head real hard," Ryan added.

"How come you're driving so slow?" Royalyn asked.

We made it to the game, which was relatively close thanks to the Cornerstone coach: he held out his two college-caliber stars most of the game to keep things competitive. He also served as the lone referee and did a fine and impartial job.

In addition, the Cornerstone folks let us spend the night at their school in Wasilla, which saved us considerable cash. We were the beneficiaries of similar sportsmanship and hospitality in earlier games against Cantwell and Glacier View — opposing fans cheering loudly for our team, post-game feasts, a free place to stay — and such warmth made these trips most rewarding. I wondered later if small town citizens elsewhere are as courteous to rival teams, or if this is a treasure found only in Alaska.

After dropping off our gear at Cornerstone, we went to dinner at a nearby Taco Bell. I regretted this culinary choice soon after we were back on the road and heading to a shopping mall. Sniffing out a teachable moment, Ole noted that gas can be both a liquid and a vapor, and, at that very moment, the van held an abundance of both! The vaporous gas volume was no doubt increased by a competition honoring the loudest and longest . . . pressure cookers.

I felt like I was driving a Port-o-Potty.

We lost a couple more games in Anchorage and went for shopping spree at Dimond Mall, a merchandise Mecca for kids from a remote village. We were planning to stay the night and show the kids more of Anchorage, but a snow-storm moving in changed our minds, and we drove back to Tetlin.

The last few miles, when we were double-teamed by Tetlin Road and Fatigue, were the toughest. It was after mid-night when I headed the van down the final descent into the village, the same hill that makes for wonderful sledding. Suddenly we hit an ice patch, tilted precariously and slid toward a stand of spruce.

"Don't panic, John!" Angela yelled.

"Get off the brake!" Ole shouted.

Working as a principal, I learned that it's important to heed the advice of students and staff members, especially when their faces are contorted with fear. I followed instruc-tions and managed to keep the van upright and miss most of the trees. A few minutes later I guided the van into the village, thus ending our odyssey.

This is the real contest here: getting the kids safely to and from games and activities in spite of poor weather and long distances. The final score is a trivial consideration when the van begins sliding toward the elephant graveyard.

We made it home. And in that sense—and that sense only—we were enjoying a perfect season.

The van was kept at the Gateway district offices, and the last time I used it was my last day in the district's em-ploy. After leaving Tetlin on an afternoon plane, I went over-board celebrating my survival at the Tok Lodge; it was the wee hours when I stumbled outside. I had to be at the dis-trict office early to do my final paperwork, and it seemed ludicrous to pay the summer tourist rates for a hotel room.

I was walking by the district offices and thinking about pitching my tent under a tree when I saw The Great White Elephant Van parked behind the buildings; as luck would have it, the door was open. I crept inside for a few fitful hours of sleep on one of the bench seats.

My suffering was predictable and terrible when I woke in the morning. An administrator was walking by, fresh from breakfast, when I slung open the van door and lost my dinner. Scared the hell out of the poor bastard. I was just happy he didn't have a recruit with him: *And this is our outgoing Tetlin principal, he'll be pleased to answer any questions you may have!*

I spent much of the summer teaching in a program at the University of Alaska in Fairbanks. Then I had the urge to roam again. I have a rule about never owning more things than I can reasonably fit into my car, so it was easy to pack up and head down the Alcan.

While I considered driving all the way to Florida for a dramatic change of scenery, I decided in the end to sample life in the Puget Sound area. I remembered reading an essay by E.B. White in which he recommended a sailboat as a cure for the restless man, so I bought a twenty-five-footer called *Morning Sun* and moved aboard.

That's my Alaska story. A capsule summary might read, "Scaled short summits, met fine folks, learned invaluable lessons and experienced buckets o' joy." Not such a wild adventure in some eyes, but it worked for me—and it may not be over. Given my wandering tendencies, I may light out again sometime for the land that so often occupies my thoughts and dreams.

About the Author

John Foley is a high school teacher and basketball coach living in Everett, Washington. He worked as a newspaper reporter in the Chicago suburbs and Alaska for almost ten years, covering sports, police, features and any other beat that didn't require him to attend sanitary sewer meetings.

Foley left the *Anchorage Times* after two years to pursue a teaching career, and he subsequently taught in the Yupik Eskimo village of Gambell and the Athabascan Indian village of Tetlin. An avid traveler, he has hitchhiked through most of North America and Western Europe. He married his second wife, Julie, in April 2002, and currently enjoys hiking in the Cascades and kayaking on Puget Sound.